U.S. Imperialism

U.S. IMPERIALISM
THE SPANISH-AMERICAN WAR TO THE IRANIAN REVOLUTION

BY
MANSOUR FARHANG

SOUTH END PRESS BOSTON, MA

Library of Congress Card Number: 81-50136
ISBN 0-89608-094-3 (paper)
ISBN 0-89608-095-1 (cloth)

Cover design by Ann L. Raszmann
Iran cover photo by Randy Goodman
Index prepared by Deana Fowler
Typeset by Larry Goldbaum
Production by the South End Press Collective
Printed by the workers at
Banta Book Co., Menasha, WI.

SOUTH END PRESS
BOX 68 ASTOR STATION
BOSTON, MA 02123

DEDICATION

To Abolhassan Banisadr
My Friend and the First
President of My Country

ACKNOWLEDGMENTS

I am grateful to my friends and colleagues William A. Dorman, Ernest Isaacs, John C. Livingston, Emily Wright, Jerry Tobey, Joan Moon and Salley Wagner at California State University, Sacramento whose criticism and comments on each chapter of the manuscript gave me intellectual inspiration as well as substantive and stylistic guidance in writing this book. Pat Walker, who was my editor at South End Press, also made an important contribution. I am also thankful to my teacher Professor Fred Warner Neal of Claremont Graduate School, who, upon listening to my views on U.S. foreign policy in a graduate seminar, kindly accused me of mixing politics with Protestant ethics. I agreed, of course, but added that Protestant ethics were actually inherited from Abraham, who, as a shepherd, was the first prophet of the people. I thank my wife Goli and children Mark, Sean and Lili for their love, encouragement and friendship.

TABLE OF CONTENTS

FOREWARD
BY RICHARD FALK

In the few weeks since my introduction was set into type spectacular developments in Iran have altered the character of the Iranian Revolution in a manner that bears directly on the life of Mansour Farhang. When he and I originally discussed the tone and content of the introduction a year ago, we felt that a certain discreetness was necessary, given the ongoing battle for influence between the Islamic Republican Party and the Bani Sadr forces. As a result, criticism of the I.R.P. leadership and of the excesses of the Iranian Revolution were to some extent muted, and no judgement was passed upon Ayatollah Khomeini's role as leader of the revolution.

In this brief interim, Farhang has moved from being a prominent member of the inner circle of the President of the Islamic Republic to being a hunted man, apparently wanted for crimes against the state. His house in Teheran has been reported surrounded by revolutionary guards. I have not had direct contact with Mansour Farhang during this period, and so it is entirely on my own responsibility that I add some comments at this point, both to put the Iranian Revolution in clearer perspective and to write with less tact than seemed prudent at the time the introduction was originally drafted.

In June, 1981 Ayatollah Ruhollah Khomeini reentered active Iranian politics with these fiery words: "Everybody should know that when I feel danger to the Islamic Republic and Islam, I will not sit back and advise...." Subsequent events have shown that Khomeini's words and presence still hold sway over the turbulent dynamics of the Iranian Revolution. And yet Khomeini's dominance is clearly not sufficient to produce the kind of unity in post-Shah Iran that was fashioned in the last months of the struggle against the Shah.

During June, amid revived rumors of Khomeini's declining health, the Iranian Revolution experienced two shockwaves. First, Abdolhassan Bani Sadr, overwhelmingly elected the first President of Iran in January, 1980, was summarily dismissed from office and declared an enemy of the revolution. He and his close advisors are wanted now by revolutionary authorities in Teheran to face criminal charges that would almost certainly lead to his execution. Indeed, street mobs in Teheran have been shouting "Bani Sadr must be 100 percent executed" in recent demonstrations. It seemed that Bani Sadr's fall from power, which was endorsed by Khomeini on June 22, represented a complete victory for Ayatollah Mohammad Beheshti and his Islamic Republican Party. This conclusion seemed confirmed by the failure of the anti-I.R.P. forces to produce any mass pro-Bani-Sadr demonstrations of protest.

The second shockwave was a series of terrorist incidents culminating in the dramatic June 28th explosion at the I.R.P. headquarters in Teheran, timed to coincide with the weekly meeting of the party leadership. Seventy-four I.R.P. notables were killed, including Beheshti, who was assumed to be the most powerful person in Iran after Khomeini, the man who had largely engineered Bani Sadr's demise. Four cabinet members and twenty-seven members of parliament perished in the blast as well. Only by apparent chance did the second and third-ranking leaders of the I.R.P., Hojetoleslam Hashemi Rafsanjani (speaker of the Majlis) and Prime Minister Muhammad Ali Rajai, escape death; both were mysteriously called from the meeting just minutes before the massive explosion.

In the special context of Shi'ia Islam, the death of Beheshti and other party leaders may be expected to enhance the moral stature of the I.R.P. Nothing is more venerated by Iranian Shi'ites than death by martyrdom, and such a death tends to vindicate the victim's path as God-chosen. At Beheshti's funeral the June 28th explosion was predictably compared to the murder of Hussein and seventy-one of his relatives and followers at Karbala, Iraq in the year 680. Hussein was the second son of Ali, who was the founder of the Shi'ites and son-in-law of the prophet Mohammad, and the day of his murder by the rival Sunni caliph has been celebrated for centuries as the great day of mourning in the Shi'ite sacred calendar, the annual climax of devotion for a religious person. More than one million Iranians showed up at the Behesht-e-Zara cemetary for the Beheshti funeral, the greatest outpouring of support for the clerical leadership since the revolution.

Despite these indications of mass support for the I.R.P., there are signs of continuing stress. Further terrorist incidents have been reported. The enemies of the I.R.P. seem to be working together for the first time since the Shah was driven from the country. Especially significant in this regard is the joining of forces between the Bani Sadr secularists and the Mujahedeen Islamic left. No one can reliably assess the real relation of forces, many imponderables remain, but the lines seem more cleary drawn between the I.R.P. and the opposition than before Bani Sadr's dismissal.

The Iranian scene is currently as inflamed as at any time since the departure of the Shah in January, 1979. A new wave of arrests and executions has occurred. In this latest outburst of governmental terrorism, more than 150 Iranians have been summarily sent before firing squads, mainly individuals associated with far-left groups, especially the Islamic socialist guerrilla organization Mujahedeen-e Khalq. The prisons are full of political prisoners. Khomeini has called on all Iranians to consider themselves henceforth as "members of the intelligence organization" and to report upon or even arrest anyone who might be an enemy of the Islamic Republic. Bani Sadr, on his part, has given an interview from hiding in which he implores Iranians "to resist in every way and at all times." The stage seems set for an internal struggle that seems likely to remain at this intense level despite the fact that Iran remains in some sense at war with Iraq and has not been able to repel Iraqi forces from its territory.

Only a fool would offer an overall interpretation of what to expect next in Iran, but a look at some specific features may help us understand the evolving situation. For reasons not yet disclosed, Beheshti and the I.R.P. leadership decided to move in on Bani Sadr in early June so as to unify their control over the governing process. Khomeini was persuaded to support this move even though only a month earlier he had still been praising Bani Sadr as "a man of the people" with all the qualities suitable for the presidency of the Islamic Republic. Why would Khomeini turn on this man, who was a devout son of an ayatollah, who had been his closest advisor in Paris, and who was himself dedicted to the creation of an Islamic Republic?

Khomeini may well have acted as he did to achieve some kind of unified leadership for the Islamic Republic while he was still alive. He had earlier mainly stayed out of the I.R.P.-Bani Sadr struggle urging each side to work for reconciliation and unity (although it seems that after the Iraqi invasion of September, 1980, Bani Sadr lost regular access to Khomeini and was being gradually discredited as a leader through Beheshti's machinations). Khomeini probably became convinced that Bani Sadr couldn't work with the I.R.P., that the I.R.P. enjoyed the overwhelming support of the revolutionary masses, and that, if a choice had to be made, the revolution was in better hands with the clergy-led I.R.P. than with the Western-educated intellectuals who formed the Bani Sadr inner circle.

Khomeini was not alone in this assessment. None other than William Sullivan, the last U.S. ambassador in Iran, has endorsed this view. Writing before Beheshti's death but after Bani Sadr's demise, Sullivan argues that Bani Sadr "had no power base, and...[h]is qualifications as a political leader were never conspicuous and, in the end, he was bound to fail." In this context, Sullivan then thought Beheshti had the best chance to stabilize the revolution in a way that might prove reasonably congenial for the United States.

Besides Sullivan's views, there were many indications of an emerging pro-I.R.P. tilt in the United States Government, including reports of secret contacts with Beheshti and indications that banks and corporations believed that business operations could resume in Iran if the I.R.P. could achieve control. Recently renewed U.S. purchases of Iranian oil also had as their effect the clear strengthening of the I.R.P. position in Iran. It is undoubtedly not a matter of Washington exactly liking the I.R.P., but rather preferring anti-Communist stability to the unpredictable drift of an uresolved power struggle that might produce opportunities for the left. Oddly enough, Bani Sadr, despite his reputation as a moderate and his opposition to the hostage diplomacy, might have been seen in Washington as the greater of two evils. Compared to the I.R.P., his approach was definitely anti-superpower, anti-international capital, left-leaning.

Of course, such a view of U.S. preferences is conjectural and confusing. In Iran, everyone from Khomeini on down is blaming the United States these days for the anti-I.R.P. terrorism. After the Iranian Majlis declared Bani Sadr politically incompetent by a vote of 177-1, Rafsanjani told a crowd waiting outside that: "From now on Mr. Bani Sadr is eliminated from the Islamic Republic. Switch your slogans toward America." Iranian specialist William O. Beeman speculates rather convincingly that the insistence on blaming outsiders arises from the view that an acknowledgement of the actuallity of internal opposition would weaken the Khomeini-I.R.P. grip on the governing process. Besides, it is always popular in Iran to blame misfortune on foreign powers. And indeed, in this century the Soviet Union, Great Britain and the United States have often been responsible for Iran's bad experiences.

One thing is clear. The I.R.P. and Khomeini regard the Iranian left, especially the Mujahedeen, which has a large popular following, as their main internal enemy. Bani Sadr also kept his distance from these left groups while President. He has now moved into some kind of oppositional alliance with them, which includes accepting their personal protection for his well-being. He has thrown in his lot decisively, since going into hiding, with even the anti-Khomeini elements of the original revolutionary coalition that overthrew the Shah.

It is still far too early to speak of a civil war or even of left-right struggle for control of the revolution (the Tudeh Party of the Communists remains, for instance, staunchly pro-I.R.P., pro-Khomeini). What can be said at this point is that Khomeini remains the clearly dominant force in the Persian-speaking center of the country (accounting for 50% of the population), and that the I.R.P. has now emerged as the exclusive instrument by which Khomeini expects to institutionalize the revolution. Elections scheduled for July 28 to select a new President and 40 new members of the Majlis (including replacements for those killed) are expected, as a matter of course, to be won overwhelmingly by the I.R.P. Either Rajai or Rafsanjani is likely to be the next President of Iran, enjoying uncontested power over the apparatus of government in Teheran.

Such a result, however, will not produce stability or bring the revolutionary process to a halt. It is not clear, for one thing, that the I.R.P. will hold together in the absence of Beheshti. The I.R.P. is itself a coalition with a spectrum of tendencies from pragmatic to fanatic. Some informed observers think that Beheshti, at the time of his death, was ready to move next against the far-right elements in the I.R.P. as part of his quest for control over the political life of the Islamic Republic. Another problem will involve the armed opposition of the underground left with its enormous base of support among the minority peoples who live around the entire periphery of Iran, including especially the several million Azerbajanis and Kurds.

Of course, also in the background is the Iraqi timebomb and the uncertain political role of the Iranian armed forces. For now the Iranian military seems content to follow Khomeini's directive to stay out of politics, but if the Imam dies or the Iraqis move, then the military may well back an anti-I.R.P. coup of some kind. And, finally, there is the evident I.R.P. dependence on Khomeini's survival. Khomeini's own grandson said a few weeks ago that "90 percent of Iran's clergy support Bani Sadr." Whether hyperbole or not, it is not clear whether the I.R.P. without either Beheshti or Khomeini would be able to maintain sufficient unity to retain control over the internal political situation, much less to stabilize the revolution.

Despite the confusion, some elements seem quite clear. Barring additional shockwaves, the I.R.P. will remain in full formal control for the time being and will continue to push the Iranian Revoluion even further in the direction of religious fascism, persecuting severely all who deviate either socially or politically, even to the slightest degree. In the most recent period there have been indications of intensifying pressures on the Bahais, including a surge of executions. Khomeini seems certain to back this new wave of repression, possibly with some misgivings, possibly not, and the United States is not likely to oppose seriously such a drift. If Khomeini dies all bets are off, and a real civil war could easily erupt with some complicated, possibly unexpected, alignments emerging.

Provided that the I.R.P. can produce some adequate leadership on its own, Khomeini is likely to once more withdraw from the forefront of Iranian politics. Not only is he very old, and possibly quite infirm, but his image of leadership has been a confined one all along, limited to intervening when, in his view, the political process of the Islamic Republic required his reinforcement. One great disappointment with Khomeini's leadership has been his failure to oppose the various revolutionary excesses of the most extreme fundamentalists. As a result, the Iranian Revolution has become, in its way, as arbitrary and repressive with respect to the rights of its opponents as was the Shah at his tyrannical worst. Khomeini must bear the burden of blame for this betrayal of the democratic side of the revolutionary vision, but there is not the slightest sign that he regards these regressive developments as a betrayal.

As of now, pro-Shah forces are not relevant to the political future of Iran, nor are the overtly pro-Western exile elements associated with the liberal Prime Minister of the Pahlavi period, Shahpour Bakhtiar. Despite some wishful thinking in conservative circles, most Iranians seem not at all prepared to revive the monarchy by inviting the Shah's son back to rule the country.

Similarly, the Soviet Union and the Moscow-aligned Tudeh Party do not seem to be factors in the current situation. The Soviet Union seems to have its hands full in Afghanistan and Poland. The Tudeh Party, which is considered well-organized but rather small, has not wavered at all in its support for the Khomeini-I.R.P. line. It is the only party of the traditional left that has been generally tolerated so far, but recently the Tudeh's newspaper was banned. Later on, in the event that the I.R.P. disintegrates or is faced with a rising tide of domestic opposition, both the Soviet Union and the Tudeh Party might be expected to exert a more independent influence, especially among the Kurds and Azerbajanis in the North.

Perhaps the most accurate assessment of the near future for Iran was made by Hajatoleslam Mohammed Montazeri (son of Ayatollah Hussein Ali Montazeri, the probable successor to Khomeini as the spiritual leader of the Islamic Republic) in an interview with French journalist Eric Rouleau, given less than 24 hours before he died in the June 28 explosion: "Executions will go on. We will be firm and expeditious, whatever the criticism against us from abroad. World opinion should try to understand us. Iran is in a state of revolution and, in addition, is a country at war, beseiged on all sides by allies of the United States who seek our downfall." The death of Beheshti has only accentuated these sentiments of being inwardly and outwardly embattled, as well as perpetuating the grip of an anti-American paranoia. The sublime irony here is, of course, that the United States Government may still, as suggested, regard the I.R.P. as being its best hope for an acceptable Iran!

So far at least 1750 persons have been executed in Iran with virtually no due process under the auspices of the Islamic Republic—enemies from the Shah's rule, opponents and critics of the new order, and a variety of petty offenders of the Islamic code of conduct (prostitutes, homosexuals, drug dealers, adulterers). While condemning these excesses, are we yet in a position to condemn the revolutionary process itself? Or is condemnation even a meaningful stance in relation to a great political upheaval of this sort?

I am reminded of Thomas Jefferson's two successive responses to the French Revolution. Writing as late as 1793 in a letter to William Short, Jefferson observed that "...The tone of your letters had for some time given me pain, on account of the extreme warmth with which they censured the proceedings of the Jacobins of France." Jefferson went on to note: "In the struggle which was necessary many guilty persons fell without the forms of trial, and with them some innocent. These I deplore as much as anybody, and shall deplore some of them to the day of my death. But I deplore them as I should have done had they fallen in battle." Jefferson then, in a remarkable passage, drew a sharp distinction between the excesses he deplored and the revolutionary process he continued to applaud. "My own affections have been deeply wounded by some of the martyrs of this cause, but rather than it should have failed I would have seen half the earth desolated."

Writing more than 24 years later, this time in a letter to a French friend, M. Barbe de Marbois, Jefferson passed a far harsher judgement: "...When I left France at the close of '89, your revolution was, as I thought, under the direction of able and honest men. But the madness of some of their successors, the vices of others, the malicious intrigues of an envious and corrupting neighbor, the tracasserie of the Directory, the usurpations, the havoc, and the devastations of your Attila, and the equal usurpations, depredations and oppressions of your hypocritical deliverers, will form a mournful period in the history of man, a period of which the last chapter will not be seen in your day or mine, and one which I still fear is to be written in characters of blood."

History has accelerated, but even so the Iranian reality has not yet hardened in the way that the French had by the time of Jefferson's 1817 assessment; we may yet perhaps hope that the Iranian Revolution will stop short of devouring itself altogether.

In reflecting upon Jefferson's altered view of the French Revolution it seems especially important to emphasize at this moment his condemnation of "the equal usurpations, depredations and oppressions of your hypocritical deliverers," alongside his eventual condemnation of revolutionary excess. Iran needs no hypocritical deliverers. The process of national revolution is only further distorted by intervention from without. Either the intervention succeeds, as it did in Arbenz's Guatemala, Allende's Chile, Nagy's Hungary or Dubcek's Czechoslovakia and the clock of history is wound back tighter. Or the intervention fails, as in Lenin's Soviet Union, Mao's China, Castro's Cuba and the revolutionary leadership feels confirmed in the view that its internal enemies seek to destroy the revolution and must be dealt with ever more harshly.

In the meantime, Mansour Farhang, author of this fine book, is in grave danger. His peril, an outgrowth of his love of country and freedom, is itself an expression of Iran's tormented politics. We await his further testimony, but for now we can learn from his probing critique of the U.S. imperial saga.

July 15, 1981
Richard Falk

Author's Preface

U.S. Imperialism: An Outsider's View from the Inside

In 1953, when Prime Minister Mohammad Mossadeq was overthrown by the CIA-engineered coup, I was a sixteen year old high school student in Tehran. Mossadeq was the leader of the National Front, an anti-imperialist coalition of a number of small political parties, the bazaar merchants, the progressive religious leaders and the liberal-left intelligentsia.

The unifying objective of the National Front was to nationalize the Anglo-Iranian oil company and end British interference in the affairs of the country. The Tudeh Party (the Communist Party of Iran) was the only competitor of the National Front in translating general dissatisfaction with the social order into an effective force.

During World War II the Iranian army had been aided by United States advisors, and later was provided with equipment and training. Having entered the Iranian scene, the United States steered the National Front forces against the British while continuing to support the Shah and the army. The real competitor of the United States in post-World War II Iran was not the Soviet Union or Communism, but Great Britain. The strategy of the United States in the Iranian crisis was to replace the British as the dominant foreign power in the country, politically and economically. This big power rivalry in Iran was a principal factor shaping the political events of the post-World War II period.

Mossadeq won his battle against the British and became Prime Minister, but this victory was the beginning of a confrontation between the forces demanding fundamental social change and the Shah as the personification of the traditional socio-political order. Mossadeq was opposed by both the right wing (the landlords, the Court, conservative religious leaders and most of the high-ranking military officers) and the Tudeh Party, which, following the Soviet line, regarded him as a front for U.S. imperialism. While the Tudeh Party was better equipped, both ideologically and organizationally, than the National Front for mobilizing a challenge to the power structure, its leaders were so preoccupied with the realm of ideology that they acted against their own interests.

The post-World War II version of the Communist ideology in Iran dictated that unconditional support for the Soviet Union came before everything else. Yet, during the same period, the Soviet Union was offending the anti-imperialist sentiment by opposing the nationalization of Iranian oil and demanding oil concessions in northern Iran as a price for withdrawing their troops from Azarbaijan.

Thus, the opposition of the Tudeh Party and the Stalinist Soviet Union to the government of Mossadeq was sustained and systematic. The Tudeh newspapers used to describe Mossadeq as the "running dog of imperialism." After the 1953 coup the Tudeh leaders stopped their attacks on Mossadeq but continued their propaganda against some of the influential elements within the National Front. The Tudeh Party, being the only organized force capable of underground activity, called for a coalition of all anti-imperialist elements against the new regime. The National Front groups unanimously rejected this invitation as a deception and condemned the Tudeh leaders for contributing to the conditions under which the coup could take place. One year after the coup, when I was arrested for distributing anti-regime leaflets, I found the arguments between the Tudeh members and the National Front elements continuing in prison.

I began my college education in the United States in the spring of 1960. I took my first course in international relations at a California State Junior College. The instructor was a liberal Democrat whose heart was with Adlai Stevenson but whose contempt for Richard Nixon had made Kennedy a more promising candidate to him. One day in class, while discussing United States interests in the Middle East, the instructor used the example of the 1953 Iranian crisis and referred to Mossadeq as the pro-Communist Prime Minister of Iran at the time. It was the first time that I had heard such a description of Mossadeq. I was so agitated by the inaccuracy of the statement that even my insecurity with English did not prevent me from asking for evidence. To my sadness, I found the instructor to be completely uninformed about the Iranian affairs of the post-World War II period. His passing reference to "pro-Communist Mossadeq" was an impression he had been carrying with him from reading about the Iranian crisis of 1953 in the newspapers and news magazines of the time.

I undertook my first research project by going over the issues of *Time*, *Newsweek*, and *U.S. News and World Report* from 1951 to 1953 in order to find out how these publications portrayed the National Front and its popular leader. What I learned from these magazines was very different from what I had seen and heard at home, in the neighborhood, in school, in prison and in the streets of Tehran. When Mossadeq took office *U.S. News and World Report* regarded him as an "international laughing stock." The magazine had no doubt that "Moscow backed Mossadeq, helped him when he needed it, counted on him to clear the way for a Communist takeover." *Newsweek* was fond of calling Mossadeq the "old Mossy." On March 9, 1953, *Newsweek* declared that "the situation is such that the West may at any instant face the choice of occupying south Iran or watching the entire country go Communist by default."

In 1951, when the United States still perceived Mossadeq as a useful instrument in ending the dominant role of Great Britain in Iran, *Time* was generous enough to describe Mossadeq as an "honest fanatic who is hard to deal with, but preferable to the Communist Tudeh Party which might take over Iran if he should fall." In 1952, *Time* chose Mossadeq as Man of the Year, but the caption under Mossadeq's cover picture read: "He oiled the wheels of chaos." The cover article on Mossadeq began by claiming that "behind his grotesque antics lay great issues of peace or war, progress or decline, which affect many lands far beyond his mountains." I felt sympathetic toward my political science instructor. The distortions were presented in such a matter-of-fact way that readers could very easily develop an impression of Prime Minister Mossadeq as a weeping, irrational fanatic and an opportunist politician with obvious pro-Communist tendencies.

This sad experience taught me that the existence of freedom and resources does not necessarily make the press coverage of human affairs fair or intelligent. Such an observation might sound naive now but at the time it was a minor crisis in my educational growth. If you live your politically conscious life in a police state, you are bound to develop too much faith in the relationship between freedom of expression and the desire to search for truth.

In my initial search for an answer to the question of why the United States' image of my country's hero was so mutilated, I found some analysts who attributed the distortions to lack of experience and understanding on the part of journalists. Others explained the unfair portrayal of Mossadeq in the context of the anti-Communist paranoia of the early 1950s. This contention, upon investigation, turned out to be no more plausible as a total explanation than the claim of reporters' inexperience with the affairs of Iran.

Although U.S. ignorance of Iran and the Cold War rivalry contributed to the misperception of Iranian affairs, these were not the principal factors in the determination of U.S. policies toward the National Front and its popular leader. I reached this conclusion after my original curiosity about my instructor's distorted view of Mossadeq led me, step by step, to make the study of imperialism, particularly U.S. imperialism, a continuing part of my academic/political life. The study of U.S. imperialism that follows is a product of my search for those factors influencing U.S. policies in Iran. It gradually became, as well, a study of consciousness.

All scientists assume some form of unity exists in the subject of their investigation. They cannot, however, all use the same method to comprehend the supposed unity. "Hard scientists" check their findings by experiments. Social scientists do not always have this opportunity because they go beyond the data of perception and indulge in rational thought and speculation. But they all proceed from the assumption that the physical or social universe is intelligible and that it is possible to find a set of relations which can explain its reality. This assumption is indispensible to any meaningful conceptualization of humanity and nature.

There is an interplay between social being and consciousness. Just as nationalism requires a national consciousness for its activation, imperialism needs for its sustenance an imperial consciousness. Since consciousness consists of the totality of attitudes, opinions, and sensitivities, any useful analysis of imperialism has to go beyond the empirical reality. It must include norms and valuations as well as factual evidence. Thus, all analyses of imperialism carry a built-in reference to the general philosophy of the analyst. I must admit that I have no claim to objectivity as the term is popularly defined. I know I am not free from the influence of tradition (the previous literature in the field of inquiry), environment (the entire social milieu), and my personal history, constitution and inclinations. Objectivity is the recognition of one's subjectivity. I hope this recognition has enabled me to overcome my prejudices in the treatment of contrary facts and ideas.

INTRODUCTION

IMPERIALISM IN CRISIS

BY RICHARD FALK

Mansour Farhang has written a challenging, provocative, thoroughly persuasive account of the course of U.S. imperialism. It is a story we need to know, especially at this time, when we seem to be preparing the military and ideological grounds for new and dangerous imperial adventures. Farhang's critique of imperialism combines the nuanced sensitivity of someone familiar with U.S. political culture through a period of long residence in this country with the detached stance of an outsider whose emotional center of gravity remains fixed in a non-Western society.

In this Introduction I propose to extend Farhang's more general concerns to the specific context of the Iranian Revolution. Such an emphasis seems especially appropriate because Mansour Farhang, in his brief tenure as an Iranian diplomat representing revolutionary Iran in Washington and later at the United Nations, was directly involved in this critical encounter between the imperial energies of the United States and the anti-imperial forces of the Third World. My intention is both to consider this encounter and to raise some questions about the humanistic content of the Iranian Revolution. It is important, in this respect, to distinguish the flow of history that gives such a strong impetus to revolutionary nationalism at this time from the ethical appraisal of outcomes of particular revolutions. On the one side, it seems evident that efforts to arrest this historical flow by way of counter-revolutionary violence are inevitably regressive. On the other side, however, the successful outcome of a given struggle for national self-determination does not assure the triumph of virtue; revolutionary results are not immune from humanistic scrutiny, even if due acount is taken of the difficult post-revolutionary setting in which external and internal threats may jeopardize to a significant degree the political independence and even the territorial integrity of the revolutionary country. Such a basic distinction between revolutionary process and specific outcome applies with special force to our understanding of developments in Iran over the past five years.

Nevertheless, from the broad outlook of contemporary history, especially from the perspective of the United States, the crucial question of the day is the extent to which our military prowess will be used once again for the unqualified defense of what Farhang calls a "transnational system of privilege," the blood and guts of the imperial game. As Americans we need to worry about the sacrifices being exacted by such a militaristic foreign policy, both for our citizenry and for foreign peoples. We need, as well, to ask for whom these sacrifices are being exacted, or, put differently, who benefits in what respects from the development of new imperial game plans in the nuclear age. The answer to such an inquiry throws us back upon our domestic political scene, including the extent to which our entire system is being held captive by militarist and elite corporate forces aligned with the overseas beneficiaries of an imperial foreign policy.

On these bases, I propose to consider the preliminary effects of the Iranian Revolution on the main lines of argument and analysis advanced by Mansour Farhang's book. First of all, some comments on the imperial heritage that shapes to such a large extent, even if unacknowledged, the political identity of the United States on the world stage. Secondly, some consideration of the U.S. response to the specific challenge of the Iranian Revolution. Thirdly, a preliminary assessment of the achievements and disappointments of post-Shah Iran. Fourthly, a few speculations about the new lines of encounter between a Reagan-led United States and the Third World. And, finally, a note on Mansour Farhang's notable record as a diplomat of revolutionary Iran acting in the difficult circumstances of a United States inflamed by the embassy seizure and hostage taking.

The Imperial Heritage

Shortly before facing one of the Shah's firing squads back in 1971, Ali Milhandust, a young Iranian activist, wrote a farewell note to his parents declaring his experience "just another proof...that no human relationship is possible between imperialism and the peoples of the world," adding that "the only kind of relationships that can exist between them are either struggle or submission."[1] It follows from such an assessment that the imperial leadership will seek over and over again, by one means or another, to assure that imperial structures of domination persist and adapt, while anti-imperial movements will search ceaselessly for tactics to dissolve these structures.

As long as the structures persist, then, the imperial elite will not learn, indeed refuses to learn, from its defeats, much less from the human costs of its various campaigns. It should, therefore, not occasion surprise that few U.S. citizens are troubled by the degree to which our presence on this land of ours was achieved at the cost of genocidal wars carried on against the various Indian peoples spread out across the continent. Still less is our collective conscience visibly troubled by the bloody war waged against the Filipino people at the turn of the century which caused as many as 600,000 deaths on the main island of Luzon alone. So long as the imperial forces prevail, the few dissenting voices are muted, easily discounted as the murmurings of eccentric, if not deranged, individuals of feverish conscience with no feeling for the worth of their own kind.

When the imperialist fortunes begin to wane, however, dissenting voices begin to be heard calling, at their extreme, for revolution, and thereby inviting retaliatory moves of repression. In this respect the U.S. experience in Vietnam was a turning-point in our imperial history, because in Vietnam a major imperial defeat was sustained; more than 50,000 U.S. lives were lost in a futile mission into a dark wilderness realm of the Third World. At home the fires of dissent raged, as did the impulse to staunch these fires in ruthless ways. Large sectors of the general public became confused. Those who opposed imperialism most visibly seemed to be attacking everything that the country stood for, and often they were. As a consequence many citizens with little understanding of the imperial struggle saw, perhaps correctly, their values and life style under attack. This often "silent majority" rose to the patrioteering bait dangled by opinion-makers, including political leaders and media moguls, and showed a readiness to serve the imperialist elite regardless of the adverse consequences for their own well-being. False lines were drawn around such issues as patriotism or hair length or musical taste; many ordinary people were democratically fooled once again.

In the United States the Vietnam experience has still not been fully assimilated. The internationalist and liberal East Coast leadership, with such informal power bases as the Trilateral Commission, the Council on Foreign Relations, and the Atlantic Council, agreed that the Vietnam encounter was a debacle. This conclusion exerted, at least temporarily, a demoralizing influence on imperialist energies. These groups also believed, however, that the Vietnam setback must not be allowed to diminish the U.S. global role, previously described as "the management of interdependence" and more recently as the protection of vital interests, especially Western access to Persian Gulf oil.[2] The mainstream of the Democratic Party seemed quite prepared to forget Vietnam, "to declare," in Jimmy Carter's phrasing, "the Vietnam Era over." This liberal approach, long ascendant, is now at least temporarily in eclipse, having been displaced by the overtly militarist and jingoist orientation of the Reagan mandate. Conservative, or neo-conservative, the

U.S. adopts an increasingly militarist counter-revisionist tone, insisting that U.S. citizens should look back upon the Vietnam attempt with pride, and explaining the outcome as a consequence of the half-hearted commitment to imperial victory on the part of civilian war managers. This, combined with a divisive peace movement orchestrated by alien forces, including the leadership in Hanoi and Moscow, weakened the national will to persist and prevail.[3] For these people, learning from Vietnam involves toughening up the martial sinews of imperialism in light of the more serious challenges already visible on the geopolitical horizon, above all the struggle over oil and dominion in the Middle East. This leads up to an emotional insistence never again to hold back in the course of battle with an enemy.

The United States, as has been frequently noted, has a special kind of imperial mentality—that of anti-imperialism. Its enterprises of domination need to be publicly reconciled not only with some deeply embedded imperatives of righteousness, but more obviously with a national heritage that celebrates its own anti-imperial, perhaps more correctly its anti-colonial, origins every 4th of July. The oft-intoned distinctiveness of the United States is bound up with the Declaration of Independence and the attendant endorsement of rights of self-determination. Therefore, our government generally postures as the guardian of self-determination, upholding the rights of others besieged from without or, paradoxically, from within. Recall those frequent reassurances from our leaders during the Vietnam years that the United States wanted nothing in Vietnam but the freedom of the South Vietnamese people or, earlier, the claims that our Monroe Doctrine diplomacy was intended to protect Latin America from the encroachments of European colonialism.

This inhibition upon imperial acknowledgment runs deep. It is reinforced by cultural thought-ways that dislike generalization about international affairs and are deeply suspicious of structural arguments that contend, for instance, that the United States' dominance in the world economy or in the international military hierarchy tends to shape its role as a certain type of actor. The genius of the United States, it is alleged defensively, stems from down-to-earth practicality, a problem-solving bent and a talent for "winning." Often the point is illustrated by comparing the inductive bias of U.S. common law with the deductive fixations of European code law. In foreign policy, this kind of temperament takes shelter in the *ad hoc* rhetoric of "realism" or "national interests." Such an outlook repudiates the moralistic strain of liberal internationalism. It does not claim that the United States is any better than others, but it does insist that the United States, like *any* other state, should define and pursue its interests in a sustainable fashion, insuring that the capabilities—read military power—exist to meet challenges.

Reducing the foreign challenge to a series of particulars is losing its appeal for policymakers in this country. The evidence of an adverse general situation has become too strong. Interestingly it is at last acceptable to acknowledge that the United States is, after all, an imperial power, if only to figure out how to arrest this process of imperial decline. A group of *Business Week* editors have put together a primer, intended as unsolicited advice to princes and princely aspirants, bearing the apt title, *The Decline of U.S. Power (and what we can do about it)*. Without mincing their words on the issue of national identity, these informal counselors to the state assert, "The country emerged from World War II with all the trappings of an imperial power and it has had to live with the problems of empire ever since."[4] Surely this is an accurate assessment, barring only a quibble about the word "emerged." Most of the trappings of empire, if not all, preceded World War II, although admittedly they were in partial ideological eclipse during Franklin Roosevelt's generally liberal presidency.

The special circumstance of the U.S. situation at present is, as the editors of *Business Week* note, one of *imperial decline*. The evidence of decline is very strong, and is reinforced by comparison with the features of other great empires in decline: compromised currency; negative trading accounts; social decay (crime, disintegration of family, drugs); rising dependence on military solutions; rising fears of chaos and external danger among the imperial citizenry; loss of confidence in the future; frequent change of discredited leaders; spread of cults; widespread apocalyptic prophecies; and hollow public rituals of reassurance. Yet in this circumstance, the imperialist ignores the comparison and instead seeks instruments and strategies of imperial renewal. There is no serious consideration of relinquishing the imperial role, or even of assessing the forces arrayed against it. As we overhear policy debate in this country, its preoccupation is exclusively tactical, that is, what to do to uphold our global role upon which domestic achievements and international stature are assumed to depend. There are, of course, those who face the reality of decline directly, acknowledging the central logic of imperial power, and have come forward with answers of a sort—restore the currency, strengthen even further military prowess and prerogative, and legislate private virtue. There is even a rebirth of "grand strategy," in the spirit of Alfred Mahan yet phrased on a global scale, proposing a U.S. foreign policy built around an all-oceans alliance of twenty-two anti-communist countries.[5] These "solutions" may win short-term popular backing among a majority of people in the United States as they at least seem responsive to the empire-maintaining challenge and do not neglect imperial necessities in the manner of die-hard liberals who pretend no such identity is pertinent to the U.S. reality. The liberal failure to acknowledge the dilemmas of imperial decline is deeply discrediting. The contention that we can go on as before constructing "the Great Society" while incurring growing fiscal deficits is less and less persuasive for the U.S. citizenry. Indeed we find now, at a time of growing danger of general war, a militarist mainstream consensus forming in this country about the prudence of vastly increased defense spending. The domain of public controversy is ridiculously confined to quibbles about dollar amounts and hardware priorities as if the resultant social hardships and war menace were inconsequential.

From biblical times, the downfall of political man has been consistently associated with stiff-neckedness. The imperialist is a special, extreme case of stiff-neckedness. He is stone-deaf when it comes to hearing the voices of the oppressed, heedless of warnings or signs, relentless in his persistence. As a result, imperialists often grasp the magnitude of their disease, yet do nothing helpful in the way of treatment. History is replete with stories of imperial collapse yet lacks any tales of imperial recovery. This apparent destiny of imperial collapse expresses the bitter truth of the present world situation of the United States. What is worse, the technology of imperial domination and the shape of inter-imperial rivalry is such that we now face the prospect of the transition from imperial decline to collapse in the form of a general war fought with nuclear weapons. Perhaps this threat does not imperil the survival of the species or even doom the general level of social attainment in the more modernized sectors of the world. Yet, even assuming such "best case" possibilities, the costs of this transition promise to be unprecedented in their magnitude.

Nothing better illustrates the situation depicted above in very general terms than does the U.S. encounter with the Iranian Revolution. Here we have manifest the full *unarmed* fury of the anti-imperialist adversary, including its energy, courage, cruelty and determination to remake the future. There was a time when an anti-imperialist adversary was no match for the United States or its co-imperialists, as demonstrated by the Marines swarming ashore to restore order in some Latin American country or the planes of Mussolini overpowering the helpless opposition of the Abyssinian people. The flow of history has reversed its course, however, the current moving strongly now in a mainly anti-imperialist direction. Such a reversal cannot be adequately understood in materialist or military terms; it is mainly a matter of a deepening of revolutionary fervor, as well as confidence that victory is possible if the challenger is willing to pay the price in blood and perseverence. How else are we to understand revolutionary victories against great odds in China, Cuba, Vietnam, Nicaragua and Iran? Of course, the imperial structures are still formidable, capable of counterattacking, and retain most of their traditional dominance over the resources, markets and weaponry of the world. It is precisely this persisting imperial strength, especially in the geopolitically pivotal Middle East with its enormous share of global oil reserves on which the West depends, which poses the threat of a nuclear showdown. This prospect is complicated, of course, by the interplay between the superpower imperial rivalry and the struggle against imperialism itself. Both dimensions are real, intersect, and point in the direction of war.

Significantly, Soviet imperialism, now revealing itself in Afghanistan, has also been hidden beneath an intense heritage of anti-imperial ideology. Western war-mongering notwithstanding, Soviet imperialism is also an imperialism in decline, especially given the regime's unpopularity at home combined with China's disaffection and the massive unrest in Poland and elsewhere in Eastern Europe. The encounter of two highly militarized declining imperial superpowers harboring various misperceptions about each other's intentions risks provoking a massive war harmful for the entire world. It also assures a lengthy series of smaller scale, yet ferocious, wars fought almost exclusively on Third World soil with Third World bodies. This is not idle chatter. An overwhelming number of the more than 100 wars fought since 1945, resulting in casualties of well over 10,000,000 people, have been confined to the territories of Africa and Asia.

The Iranian Revolution is occurring in the eye of this momentous imperialist storm. Its leader, Imam Ruhollah Khomeini, adamantly rejects both U.S. and Soviet imperialism. Yet Iran lies astride the Straits of Hormuz through which passes a majority of the world's traded oil and has such vast stocks of oil that it was, until the struggle against the Shah erupted, second only to Saudi Arabia as an oil exporter. For these reasons, Iran cannot be left alone by imperial forces, nor, it now seems, can it necessarily sustain its revolutionary process to enable it to become a center of anti-imperial strength in the region.

The Iranian Challenge

The U.S. response to the Iranian Revolution continues a consistent strain of counter-revolutionary diplomacy that goes back to the very beginnings of the republic, commencing with a generally hostile reaction to the French Revolution. More fundamentally, the official U.S. posture toward the struggles of others for freedom was shaped by the brutal dispossession of the

Indian and the reliance on black slaves for cheap farm labor. And still further back is the shaping influence of the outlook of European explorers and their financial backers, who conceived the rest of the world as a wilderness ripe for civilizing, that is, for taming, plundering and colonizing. It is the West alone among world civilizations that has moved out from its regional origins to destroy and supplant the civilizations of others. Frederick Turner, in his brilliant recent book *Beyond Geography: The Western Spirit Against the Wilderness*, wonders aloud whether the ultimate explanation of these predatory features of Western Civilization is not a matter of geography—a turning away from the harsh struggle for survival in the stony Middle East toward a restive quest for deliverance elsewhere, always elsewhere, always at the expense of others.[6]

The imperial mind is imbued with notions of control and dominion, and has nightmares about disorder and chaos. Because of this, the imperial reaction to the self-assertions of the subordinated social group, whether class, race, region or religion is reflexive in a primordial sense. It is more fundamentally an attempt to uphold interests in markets, resources, and investments. The U.S. relationship to the Third World is illustrative. With its anti-colonial credentials, whether deserved or not, and with the rest of the colonial world shattered by warfare, the United States after World War II appeared to retain an option to move with the revolutionary nationalist flow of history, and benefit therefrom. The failure to do so reflected, in part, the burdens of unfreedom embedded in the imperial frame of mind; there was no cultural freedom, in other words, to participate in a process that called for the relinquishing of controls. Real rivalries with the Soviet Union over the future of Europe were generalized to include the entire world. The Cold War was on, with the United States firmly in the colonial corner, although not without one eye cocked to pick up the pieces of the inevitably crumbling French and English Empires. The Soviet Union, surely not devoid of geopolitical ambitions of its own, took advantage of historic opportunities created in part by the United States' over-zealous support for "the losing side" in history. The direct action by the Soviet Union, minor compared to what was being done to help the imperial side by the United States, was used to confirm the U.S. view that the anti-imperial movement should be primarily interpreted as Soviet expansionism. Such a view, besides being ideologically inflammatory, involves a distortion of perception, gravely underestimating the autonomous historical energies that move in various revolutionary nationalist directions.

The course of encounters in Iran is indicative of this pattern. The United States first moved to get the Soviets out of northern Iran in the mid-1940s. Then, in 1953, with the assistance of British intelligence, it staged a coup to restore imperial order. This, incidentally, increased the share of Iran's oil production by major U.S. oil companies from zero to almost 50 percent. Quite a coup of its own! Restoring the Pahlavi monarch to his peacock throne, while throwing out of power a constitutional reformer like Muhammad Mossadeq, would seem like a willful violation of our own preference for relatively liberal democracy as against inherited and dynastic privilege. However, no serious protest along such lines was heard in the United States from 1953 until 1978 when the Shah's tyranny started to unravel. Indeed, the architects of "the free world," active in Washington in the 1950s scorned Mossadeq as a fanatic and xenophobe, overlooking his liberal secular ideals and acts. They were most content to help the then young Shah resume his rule, this time in a manner that would last. As we all know by now, "help" included building up a terrorizing secret police, SAVAK, that eventually established torture centers throughout Iran, as well as an extensive military assistance program.

Again in 1978, the struggle against the Shah was first ignored, then scorned and condemned. It was assumed by Washington experts on Iran that, at worst, these religious manifestations of resistance would be "handled" in the manner of 1963 when extensive protests led to thousands of government-inflicted deaths and the exile of Ayatollah Khomeini, who was perceived at the time as the main anti-Shah agitator among the upper clergy. At the end, when the demise of the Shah seemed assured, there was much speculation by U.S. leaders and their media cohorts about this strange, regressive resurgence of Islam, powered by a mysterious religious leader who had lived for years in virtual isolation, carrying on his religious life in an obscure Iraqi town. There was little appreciation and less understanding of the depth and breadth of the Iranian Revolution, a mass mobilization on an unprecedented scale that confounded Marxist class-bound ideas about struggle as well as imperial police-oriented conceptions of order. Virtually the whole Iranian population seemed united in their commitment to be rid of the Shah and "the American connection"; almost the entire urban population of Iran joined the last stages of the revoluion regardless of class, race or region. Only those few Iranians closely connected with the Shah's system of abuse and exploitation scurried abroad to safety, generally taking with them as much loot as possible.

We need not suspend criticism of what has ensued in Iran to appreciate that the mass non-violent movement of struggle waged by the Iranian people in such a courageous fashion is a glorious chapter in revolutionary history. The United States' response was predictable in tone although indecisive in substance. Early in his presidency Jimmy Carter had exempted the Shah's regime from his human rights diplomacy. Even granting practical arguments (oil, business, geopolitical allies), Carter seemed to go further than necessary, visiting Iran for mainly social purposes on New Year's Day of 1977, toasting the Shah in extravagant language as an enlightened leader loved by his people, and acting generally oblivious to either the Shah's bloody record or the rising tide of popular resistance. Having embraced tyranny so firmly it is difficult to let go, especially when the tyrant comes upon hard times. It is no wonder that Carter's failure to rescue the Shah, or at least to welcome him with open arms after his overthrow, seemed weak and disloyal to the avowedly imperial (David Rockefeller, Henry Kissinger and Richard Nixon among others).

In a sense, Carter did his best. He praised the Shah whenever he showed imperial resolve, most dramatically supporting the massacre by machine gun of several thousand unarmed demonstrators in Jaleh Square on September 8, 1978. Toward the end of that revolutionary year the U.S. president sent naval ships in the direction of Iran, menacingly threatening an intervention. Even more directly, in the closing days of the revolution an important U.S. general, then deputy commander of NATO Robert Huyser, was sent to Tehran. He was the direct representative of a concerned White House, anxious to keep the Iranian high command together and to support and develop anti-Khomeini coup scenarios. These U.S. maneuvers were well-known to the Iranian revolutionary leadership at the time, and were resented by the progressive and democratic forces which particularly needed a calm, rational political environment to achieve their ends.

It is telling that a revolution so evidently anti-Marxist and anti-Soviet would elicit such hostile reactions in Washington. Of course, the imperial legacy is powerful and shaped the non-pragmatic character of subsequent United States' conduct. There was no feasible way for the Carter Administration to turn over a new leaf in Iran and go along with the obvious will of the Iranian people, and simultaneously serve U.S. national interests in oil, peace, and Soviet containment. For one thing, the fervor of the revolution naturally embraced the Palestinian cause, thereby exposing more than ever the United States' one-sided relationship to the Arab-Israeli struggle. For another, the wandering Shah was a flaming torch for both sides. After so many crimes of state, how could he be ignored by the Iranians with their Islamic ethics of retribution? And contrariwise, after so much loyal service as a friend (Kissinger, in his memoirs, aptly remarks that the Shah was "that rarest of things, an unconditional ally"), how could the Carter Administration suddenly avert its glance?

The practical arguments for denying the Shah access to the United States were strong. Why stir trouble? Yet there were diehard Shah loyalists in the President's immediate entourage, as close in as Brzezinski, who pressed for the Shah's admission here, possibly even hoping to provoke a confrontation that could set a counter-revolutionary train in motion. As usual in the Carter years, the White House wavered, buffetted by a variety of pressures and counter-pressures. Then, under a medical pretext the Shah was admitted to the United States on Oct. 22, 1979, for allegedly imperative treatment. The claimed necessity was not independently investigated at the time, and was later proved false. Even without the medical argument the Carter Administration was on the verge of yielding to those forces pressing for the Shah's admission here. What else could poor Jimmy have done? Had Carter second-guessed the medical recommendations of David Rockefeller's private doctor and turned the Shah away under these circumstances, he would likely have been attacked as heartless and disloyal to former allies. Carter's vulnerability to the Rockefeller-Kissinger efforts was understandable, especially as members of his own inner circle supported the idea of admitting the Shah to this country. No politician is likely to commit suicide, even on behalf of national interests.

The rest of the story is quite familiar. The Shah's entry led to the November 4th Embassy seizure by several hundred militants, later identified as Students in the Line of the Imam. The occurrence became a major remobilizing experience for the faltering Iranian Revolution and was celebrated and endorsed by Khomeini as a great victory. The United States government then blustered and thundered, invoking piously, after all its misdeeds, the clear rules of international law safeguarding diplomats. Months later it put together a covert operation spectacularly designed, or at least advertised, to rescue the 53 Americans then held hostage. As we all know, the April 1980 rescue operation failed embarrassingly in the Iranian desert when three of eight helicopters malfunctioned. The incident was a tall story in tall times, but nevertheless a clear expression of U.S. political will to rescue the hostages, even if it meant killing them.

In the background all this time were the drumbeats of domestic politics on both sides. In Iran the hostage diplomacy was seized upon by the hard-line faction in the Islamic Republic Party as a litmus test of revolutionary credibility. It was also seen strategically as a way to displace the progressive and democratic elements associated with former Prime Minister Mehdi Bazargan and the popularly elected president, Abolhossein

Bani Sadr. This domestic encounter overshadowed prudence in foreign affairs (not giving the United States, Iraq and other enemies of the Iranian Revolution an excuse for intervention) and practicality at home (getting on with the urgent tasks of economic and social reconstruction after many hardship months of strikes and shutdowns).

In the United States, the hostage crisis created a dramatic opportunity for the Carter presidency to stake its claim to steady, responsible leadership. While denouncing the seizure as barbarian for the sake of public delight, the Carter people at first tried to win freedom for the hostages by sympathetic gestures of accommodation (such as the early abortive effort to send Ramsey Clark, a friendly negotiator who was, ironically, denounced by Carter at a later stage in the crisis for making an unauthorized trip for essentially the same purposes). We know, also, that throughout the crisis the State Department was playing tug-of-war with the White House and Pentagon about the proper tactics to use. The latter was more responsive to the popularity of cowboy gallantry with the home folks than it was concerned by adverse reactions in the Islamic world or among oil-dependent allies in Western Europe and Japan. Cyrus Vance, with a more discerning imperial view, resigned as Secretary of State to express his disapproval of strongarmed tactics that jeopardized the lives of the hostages, disturbed relations with principal allies, as well as endangered needlessly the position of the West in the Persian Gulf as a whole.

The dramatic denouement of the hostage crisis was climaxed by their release in the early moments of the Reagan presidency, literally on Inauguration Day, January 20, 1981. In the end, the practicalities of the Iraq-Iran War and the loss of access to Iranian assets as a result of the Carter freeze seemed decisive. The negotiations with the Carter Administration centered around financial arrangements, and Iranians made no effort at the end to reassert their earlier view that the whole affair was a reaction against prolonged U.S. intervention in Iranian internal affairs during the Shah years. From an Iranian point of view the clumsiness of the hostage release greatly compromised their ideological position vis-a-vis the United States.

Now that the hostage crisis has resolved itself, we can tentatively conclude that contradictory legacies from the past and divergent domestic political imperatives played a decisive part in shaping the post-revolutionary encounter between Iran and the United States. There is no way for the imperial snake to shed its skin all at once, nor for revolutionary agitation to relax into the normalcy of diplomatic routine. The future of the United States-Iran relationship remains in doubt, especially whether the leadership in both countries will be guided by practical considerations which would lead in the direction of normalization or by ideological compulsions which could provoke new confrontations.

The Post-Revolutionary Context in Iran

We all know that the old political models are not working, but how much better are the newer models doing? Disillusionment with state socialism in the Soviet Union and Eastern Europe is nearly universal by now. The spread of Stalinist tactics and structures to Third World communist politics has also convinced many progressive people that Marxist revolutionary victories do not necessarily produce positive results—the spectre of "the boat people" and other refugees from communism has taken its toll on world public opinion. China's seeming embrace of U.S.-styled modernization together with a foreign policy that supports reactionary patterns so long as they are anti-Soviet, has disenchanted many early supporters of the Chinese Peoples Republic. All in all, these disappointments with the socialist path have complicated the anti-imperialist struggle.

The Iranian Revolution was from the outset a welcome attack on the old models, but could it be understood in more positive terms than as a stage of struggle? The symbolism of the revolution seemed more Islamic than Iranian, although such distinctions did not exist in the minds of most Iranians during the 1977-78 period of anti-Shah upheaval. The essence of the shared goals was the overthrow of tyranny and solidarity with the poor. Beneath Khomeini's hostility to the West in general and the two superpowers in particular, there seemed to be an authentic revolutionary commitment on a global scale to the cause of the oppressed. In this respect, the intensely religious outlook of the Iranian Revolution was not a cause for concern, except to the extent that it rejected the left's secular contributions to the struggle against the Shah and augered ideological strife among the victors in Iran. The early hope was that even this conflict would be tempered by the promise of a democratic framework for competing points of view and the broad consensus about social, economic, cultural and political goals which seemingly united all elements of the victorious revolutionary forces in Iran.

Now, almost two years later, the rainbow of revolutionary victory has faded in Iran. Revolutionary unity has disappeared and some elements of authoritarian rule have re-emerged. Emblematic of the overall situation, perhaps, is the shift in position of the People's Mojahedin Organization, an Islamic socialist political formation, from the front rank of revolutionary celebrants in February 1979 to the position of enemy of the Islamic Republic by the summer of 1980. The situation in Iran remains unclear and all crystal balls seem clouded over.

The most repressive deviation from the democratic content of the original revolutionary goals occurred in the judicial sphere, where there appeared hasty, harsh justice without adequate safeguards for the accused. Many local komitehs have been reckless in their ways, punishing without due process and generating an atmosphere of intimidation. Technical abuses of Islamic codes, such as drinking, have produced floggings. Bloody justice has been administered in a seemingly arbitrary manner, most spectacularly by Ayatollah Sadegh Khalkhali, who although removed from his original role as chief of the revolutionary courts, continued for many months to operate freely as chief inquisitor of the Iranian Revolution.

Policies adopted toward non-Persian minorities have also provoked concern. Although controversy surrounds vital facts on such matters, and the reality of foreign meddling cannot be ignored, it remains the case that the response of the Islamic Republic to claims for minority rights and status has, at times, been repressive. Of course various ethnic groups in Iran, sensing the fluidity of the post-revolutionary situation, saw the moment as an opportune one to advance their maximal case for their autonomy, acting sometimes in a provocative and belligerent manner. Such ethnic assertions were, in turn, perceived "at the center" to be deeply "anti-revolutionary" and "anti-state" in their intention and effect.

At times the Iranian revolutionary leadership has seemed responsive toward minorities, going far, especially as measured by Iranian history, to meet autonomy demands. Yet there have been additional charges of abuse made by such Iranian religious minorities as the Bahais and Jews. Bahais, viewed by Shi'ia Islam as heretics, have been under constant pressure since the end of the revolution. Jews, while officially assured of a protected place in an Islamic Republic and even awarded a seat in the new Parliament, have been worried by anti-Zionist sentiments. There have been some incidents of harrassment in Iran based only on the Jewish identity of the targets. Several prominent members of the Jewish community have been executed, their cases centering on charges that they were strong, active supporters of Israel.

A further charge involves the treatment of women. The revolution, which was supported by the overwhelming majority of Iranian women, seems by now to have antagonized a significant segment of the female population. Critics of the revolutionary process in Iran contend that the inauthentic and alienating mania for western culture which was so much a part of the lives of urban middle class women in the Shah's Iran has been replaced by repressive conditions that are, in their own way, equally inauthentic and alienating. It appears that one form of irrationality has led to another. The massive participation of women in the Iranian Revolution was unprecedented in the history of Third World revolutions. Iranian women sought their freedom through the revolutionary process, but many of them now fear the loss of their elementary rights. It seems doubtful that Iranian women will acquiesce to this betrayal of their hopes; indeed, we can expect that the mass struggle by women to achieve liberation will continue in the context of the Islamic Republic.

On a general level the Islamic Republic seems to have moved in a dangerous and unfortunate direction, whether it be in relation to the ideas of the left, the secular convictions of the urban constitutionalists, or the quest for democratic prerogatives in relation to life style and cultural activities. Newspapers have been shut down, book stores raided, schools and universities made to toe the Islamic line and closed, opponents arrested or driven underground. Serious scholars and administrators have been replaced, in many reported instances, by semi-educated clerics or their lay flunkies. Despite these setbacks in the struggle to realize the democratic promise of the Iranian Revolution, it should be understood clearly, especially in view of hostile propaganda, that the range of freedom and tolerance in Iran today is far greater for most of the population than it was under the Shah.

In addition to this enumeration of abuses, there is a gathering record of ineptitude, especially in the economic sphere. Large sectors of the Iranian economy, the building and industrial trades for example, remain idle. Unemployment is high and rising. Little energy has been devoted to reviving the economy, carrying out the promises of the revolution to equalize incomes and land tenure, evolving an industrial and agricultural order responsive to Iran's needs and resource endowments, including human skills. Many ordinary Iranians suffer and the middle classes have fallen into a state of growing despair as a result of the virtually total preoccupation of the religious leadership with the most contentious aspects of its revolutionary agenda, including the quest for secular dominance. Although evidently not part of the internal power struggle, Khomeini himself has not strongly supported the process of societal reconstruction and has emphasized instead purity at home and the spread of the Iranian experience to other parts of the Islamic world. Since the onset of the Iran-Iraq War in the fall of 1980, however, Khomeini's espousal of these themes has grown more muted.

Finally, this post-Shah path of the Islamic Republic has been said to jeopardize both the gains of the Iranian Revolution and the territorial and political independence of Iran. The hostage diplomacy, while it lasted, created a massive ideological basis for U.S. intervention, indeed for the entire array of reactionary enemies of Iran. By stepping outside the protective shield of accepted international legality and morality—outside even the minimum formal content of mutual respect for sovereign rights—the ruling factions in Iran have, in effect, provided a pretext for various hostile initiatives by exiles, by neighboring states and by the superpowers, especially, so far, the United States. One has to wonder if the Iraqi invasion of September 1980 would have occurred had not the course of the Iranian Revolution resulted in so many self-inflicted wounds, including a degree of diplomatic isolation (regionally and globally) that was as unnecessary as it was imprudent.

These lines of criticism are not the whole story and need to be balanced against other features of the situation, especially the U.S. tendency to disclose only the negative side of the Iranian experience. Hostile reporting has been a dimension of the Iranian experience all along, aggravated since late 1978 by a deliberate official manipulation of the news in a manner calculated to discredit the forces victorious against the Shah and U.S. imperialism. The bad has been consistently exaggerated, the good ignored. Besides, western secularism, whether of the left, right or center, is deeply distrustful of and frightened by religious politics; because of this fear negative perceptions often tend to be mere projections. Such a provincial tendency is underscored by cultural distance, a distance extended further by the anti-western animus of Khomeini's outlook. Finally, revolutionary fervor never neatly accommodates liberal insistence on due process, fairness to enemies and rational moderation; the spirit and mood is different. The liberal critics in Iran are also likely to have stayed near or on the sidelines during the revolutionary struggle itself because it seemed "hopeless," or there was no point in being "rash" and "reckless."

There have been revolutionary achievements as well as failures in Iran since February of 1979. The Shah's structures of dependence and exploitation have been largely smashed. The role of foreign enterprise has been severely curtailed. The Iranian oil industry has been put in the service of the Iranian people and their values. Progressive ends have been served: there is no more oil for South Africa; the Palestinian cause has been promoted; Iran has consistently supported Third World anti-imperial demands. Whatever else, the foreign policy of Iran in this period has been anti-rightist, even to the point of breaking off diplomatic relations with Pinochet's regime in Chile explicitly because of its repressive character. Furthermore, the Iranian victory and Khomeini's leadership has brought to people of the Islamic faith a new conviction of their worth and power, a momentous historic achievement whose full weight has not yet been felt. Recall that at Auschwitz the word "Muslim" was used by prisoners to designate the most totally intimidated and broken-spirited inmates, whose very debasement made them immediately eligible for the gas chamber. This Islamic resurgence, personified by the sanctified figure of Ayatollah Khomeini, has struck fear into the hearts of regional tyrants and monarchs as well as worryed those, most notably Anwar Sadat, who rule their countries in a manner calculated to bring dollars and praise from the West.

Internally, also, there are achievements. Progress has been made in the agricultural sector, both toward increasing output and redistributing land to the poor. Other economic plans are in the works and may now, with the semblance, at last, of a functioning governing process, go forward with wide public support.

Elections, generally thought to be fair aside from rather rigid eligibility requirements, have been held at the local and national levels, often for the first time in decades. The 1980 presidential election, despite the disqualification of two strong opponents of Bani Sadr (neither sufficiently popular to win) seemed definitely to allow a range of candidates to compete openly for popular favor. Ayatollah Khomeini has generally acted in accordance with popular will, even in the matter of endowing his own person with supreme powers in the redrafted Constitution.

So far many revolutionary excesses have been avoided, or curtailed. Policies and practices abusive of minority rights, however lamentable in their existence, have been confined within fairly narrow limits, even with respect to Bahais and

Jews. The revolution has not yet, in the manner of major revolutions of the past, devoured its own but rather tended to cast aside and even reassimilate earlier leaders. For example, Mehdi Bazargan and Ibrahim Yazdi, members of the original moderate cabinet and for a while under intense pressure by IRP forces, have continued to play active, leading roles after falling from the pinnacles of power. So far, too, Bani Sadr has held on as president and commander of the armed forces.

The Iranian Revolution has gone forward on its own momentum, defining its structures as it proceeded. It is a mass revolution apparently scornful of constitutional rights, especially those most valued by the middle classes. It is a revolution and a political culture inexperienced, to put it mildly, in democratic governance. The Islamic identity of the movement also can be construed to support demands for vengeance and adherence to harshly specific codes of conduct. Additionally, some of the greatest revolutionary excesses have taken place as a result of decentralized, semi-rural forms of Islamic extremism that do not reflect the will or policy of the center.

Outsiders have complained about the absence of "authority structures" in Iran, about an inability to identify who was in charge. U.S. diplomats complained about this, especially during the frustrating months consumed in frantic efforts to resolve the hostage crisis. Yet this fragmentation of authority reflected a willingness of the leadership, including Khomeini, to allow the revolution to continue on its own course after the Shah's collapse. It remains premature to condemn such a course. After all, the statist orientations of leaders around the world have not succeeded in protecting human rights or achieving peaceful international relations.

Although there are many reasons to be troubled by the evolving character of the Iranian Revolution, it is too soon to pass judgment. The record is more mixed than the U.S. media allows, and the situation in Iran remains sufficiently fluid to make a progressive destiny still possible, although by no means likely, much less assured.

The Prospect of Struggle and Intervention in Post-Carter America

Eloquently Farhang addresses the central issue of anti-imperialist prospects. He sees clearly that these prospects depend for their realization upon the struggles of the oppressed and the splits among the oppressors, both inter-capitalist rivalries across boundaries and various sources of opposition within the imperial stronghold itself.

The global situation is exceedingly complex. The Soviet Union has itself become an interventionary actor in the Third World, fighting a protracted war in Afghanistan on behalf of its client regime. The election of Ronald Reagan as president, although mainly an expression of discontent with Keynes and Carter, has nevertheless provided an endorsement of sorts for an avowedly interventionist U.S. foreign policy, one that makes no pretenses about its counter-revolutionary goals. At present, this new imperial resolve is being tested in Central America, especially El Salvador, where the transnational system of privilege is entrenched in a manner that inflicts acute misery on the people of the country. This new overtness by the United States is causing some alarm even among centrist forces that are themselves opposed to left political solutions for the Third World.

Farhang helps us grasp the structural elements of this ongoing struggle, the central political drama of our age. He also develops a humanistic framework that is concerned with the actualities of various governing processes rather than with their ideological labels. The important content of liberation consists of the alleviation of economic and social privation, the realization of political independence and cultural autonomy, and the general experience of life in a manner consistent with human dignity. Such an emphasis is a constant reminder (and warning) that whether revolutions succeed or fail depends finally on whether or not they contribute to human happiness and societal self-esteem. A normative stress does not imply an embrace of individualism, but rather the adoption of a view of "humane society" that embraces both individual and group aspects, a view that is becoming necessarily global in outlook.[7]

The struggle against the transnational system of privilege

has barely begun. We no longer have the illusion that the end of colonialism assured the collapse of imperialism. A new constellation of forces has emerged, involving compliant domestic elites, counterinsurgency training and capabilities, covert operations of stabilization and destabilization, multinational corporations and transnational banks, an imperial information order, and a persisting willingness and capability by the dominant states to intervene under an ever-shifting variety of pretexts and doctrinal justifications.

The understanding and capabilities of popular forces are also growing, however, including their own dedication to genuine independence and non-alignment. The superpowers, as well as China, have been decisively discredited as guides for revolutionary processes in the Third World. In the years ahead it is likely that new directions will be taken in this central struggle against the transnational system of privilege. Mansour Farhang has given us a framework for interpreting, and welcoming, such new directions.

A Concluding Biographical Note

Against this background Mansour Farhang's book is both invaluable as analysis and revealing as to the perspective of a principal supporter of the Iranian Revolution. His own life, in a sense, is expressive of the meandering course of Iranian politics. Long active as an anti-Shah Iranian exile living in the United States, Farhang moved toward an identification with the progressive side of Islam, partly through his friendship with Ali Shariati, who has been widely hailed as "the philosopher of the Iranian Revolution." Farhang accepted and welcomed an indigenous Iranian revolution owing nothing by way of ideology to the West. He also fully realized the extent to which Khomeini's leadership enabled the mobilization of an incredibly intense level of mass support, achieving total victory with almost no reliance on armed struggle.

At the same time Farhang, as a serious student of imperialism and tyranny, became deeply troubled by the post-revolutionary reality of Iran. Despite these gathering concerns, Farhang in 1979 abandoned the security of his California academic life to serve the Iranian Revolution, first as a diplomatic advisor in its Embassy in Washington and then as its U.N. Ambassador. With exceptional ability Farhang became the leading spokesperson in the United States for the Iranian position during the hostage crisis, explaining the resentment of his people while sharing his personal qualms about the hostage diplomacy. Finally, as this tension grew too strong, Farhang resigned his diplomatic post and returned to Iran in July of 1980, still committed to realizing the democratic and progressive potential of the Iranian Revolution.

As a public official Mansour Farhang exhibited the best qualities of academic-turned-politician, qualities we in this country are unaccustomed to given our recent experiences with the cynical machinations of first Kissinger and later Brzezinski. Farhang acted as a true Iranian patriot without ever quieting his conscience into unwarranted submission or silence. He earned wide respect and a U.S. audience for his views, views which were neither apologetic for what was happening in Tehran nor, in any sense, a departure from the outlook that had earlier made Farhang such a vivid, intellectual partisan of the Iranian Revolution.

In this respect the life of the author stands squarely, almost uniquely, behind the analysis of this book. We have here a timely, original, probing critique of U.S. imperialism which sees the anti-imperialist struggle in democratic, humanist terms. Farhang's understanding of imperialism as consisting of structures of "transnational privilege" is a genuine contribution to both the theory of imperialism and that of revolution, making sense along the way of why even economically privileged classes may join the revolution to save their cultural and spiritual identities. In this central respect Farhang's approach to revolution is post-materialist in orientation.

As Americans we need every chance we can get to grasp why persisting with an imperialism still mired in an overwhelmingly materialist ethos leads us further along a nuclear blind alley. This book is one such chance to learn, and by learning to turn quickly and seriously in a life-affirming direction—that is, in the direction of post-materialist revolution.

Introduction Footnotes

1. Quoted in *Mojahed*, February 11, 1980, p. 18.

2. For a characteristic argument along these lines see Robert W. Tucker, "The Purposes of American Power," *Foreign Affairs* 59 (1980-81), pp. 241-274.

3. This line of Vietnam revisioning is persuasively depicted in Walter LaFeber, "Vietnam and the Next War," *Democracy* 1 (1981), pp. 93-103.

4. *The Decline of U.S. Power (and what we can do about it)* (Boston: Houghton Mifflin, 1980), p. 10.

5. So argued by a former CIA high official who has been prominently associated with President Reagan's foreign policy entourage. Ray S. Cline, *World Power Trends and U.S. Foreign Policy for the 1980s* (Boulder, Colo.: Westview, 1980).

6. Frederick Turner, *Beyond Geography: The Western Spirit Against the Wilderness* (New York: Viking, 1980).

7. For innovative exploration along this line see Robert Johansen, *The Human Interest and the National Interest* (Princeton: Princeton University Press, 1980).

CHAPTER 1

EVOLVING THEORIES OF IMPERIALISM

For about seventy-five years after the success of the American Revolution, the colonial possessions of the European powers were on the decline. Great Britain had to give up the American colonies, and Spain and Portugal lost their South American territories in the decades following the establishment of the United States. The big powers of Europe, to be sure, had their colonial possessions, but they were not particularly active in pursuit of new territories.

In the late 19th century the situation changed drastically. Britain, France, Portugal and the Netherlands expanded their already existing areas of imperial interest in Africa and Southeast Asia. Germany, Italy and Belgium were just becoming imperial powers. Russia, not quite in the same category as other European powers, continued its overland movement eastward. Altogether, Europeans extended their formal colonial empires by over 10 million square miles and 150 million people—a fifth of the world's land area and a tenth of its population at the time.

The colonial powers used force and the threat of force to conquer and maintain control over their new possessions.

> While small groups of competing Europeans struggled across the plains and through the swamps of Africa and Southeast Asia and sailed among the innumerable Pacific Islands, inducing the inhabitants by force or persuasion to sign treaties of protection or cession with them, the heads of state in Europe argued ceaselessly and tried to establish effective control over the great areas so tenuously acquired. A crescendo of tension and violence was reached at the end of the century with the massacre of twenty thousand dervishes by Kitchener and his British troops at Obdurman, before Khartoum, in 1898; the meeting of the French and British at Fashoda on the upper Nile, later that year, which almost brought on war between them; the war between Spain and America in 1898; the outbreak in 1899 of the three-year conflict between the British and the Boers in South Africa; and the Boxer Rebellion in China in 1900.[1]

While these developments were defended by many Europeans and Americans as the necessary and legitimate pursuit of their national interests, a number of leading liberal, socialist and communist thinkers attacked them with the purpose of uncovering and destroying their roots. It was the efforts of such critics which led to the formulation of theories of imperialism in the early part of the 20th century. The leading theoreticians of imperialism during the period developed an analysis of the *economic* necessities which drove capitalists into overseas political domination. There are three main factors in these economic explanations of imperialist expansion: 1) the need for raw materials to meet the growing demands of industrial society; 2) the need to secure new markets for the surplus products of home industries; 3) the need to find new investment areas for the surplus capital of industrial and financial concerns. Although some economic analysts of imperialism emphasize one or two of these factors, most take into account all three as the interrelated economic sources of imperialism. This does not mean, however, that the theoreticians of imperialism lack diversity of prescriptions or conflicting arguments.

J.A. Hobson was the first and most influential theoretician of imperialism in the early 20th century. He defined imperialism as "...the use of the machinery of government by private interests, mainly capitalists, to secure for them economic gains outside their country."[2] He maintained that imperialism was rooted in the failure of English capitalism to bring about an adequate distribution of income for the working classes. "The economic root of imperialism," Hobson said, "is the desire of strong organized industrial and financial interests to secure and develop, at the public expense and by the public force, markets for their surplus goods and their surplus capital. War, militarism and a 'spirited foreign policy' are the necessary means to this end."[3] Thus, imperialism is due to the impoverishment of the working class, and the resulting lack of demand for goods and services. The excess productive capacity that results in turn pushes surplus capital to seek new areas of investment. Hobson thought imperialism must be ended because it leads to war, and he used his theory to argue for market expansion and income redistribution inside England as a way of ending imperialism. Thus, he saw imperialism as a matter of choice and not the inevitable outcome of economic necessity.

Hobson also condemns the British expansion as a business policy and maintains that it "has jeopardized the entire wealth of the nation in rousing the strong resentment of other nations."[4] Then he asks, "...how is the British nation induced to embark upon such unsound business?"[5] His answer to this question constitutes the central contention of his analysis of imperialism. "The only possible answer is that the business interests of the nation as a whole are subordinated to those of certain sectional interests that usurp control of the national resources and use them for their private gain."[6] Hobson proceeds to prove empirically that although British "...imperialism has been bad business for the nation, it has been good business for certain classes and certain trades within the nation."[7]

Imperialism, therefore, is against the "real interests" of the vast majority of the peoples, both in the imperialist and imperialized societies. As Hobson writes, "...the vast expenditure on armaments, the costly wars, the grave risks and embarrassments of foreign policy, the stoppage of political and social reforms within Great Britain, though fraught with great injury to the nation, have served well the present business interests of certain industries and professions."[8] Thus, the sectional interests "...are the enemies of national safety and the commonwealth."[9] It follows that the imperialist wars are "...irrational from the standpoint of the whole nation, but they are rational enough from the standpoint of certain classes in the nation."[10] However, Hobson does not consider this irrationality to be rooted in capitalism. He writes,

> A completely socialist State which kept good books and presented regular balance-sheets of expenditure and assets would soon discard Imperialism; an intelligent laissez-faire democracy which gave duly proportionate weight in its policy to all economic interests alike would do the same. But a State in which certain well-organized business interests are able to outweigh the weak, diffused interest of the community is bound to pursue a policy which accords with the pressure of the former interests.[11]

Hobson places the financier in the center of the imperialist network.

> In view of the part which the non-economic factors of patriotism, adventure, military enterprise, political ambition, and philanthropy play in imperial expansion, it may appear that to impute to financiers so much power is to take a too narrowly economic view of history. And it is true that the motor-power of imperialism is not chiefly financial: finance is rather the governor of the imperial engine, directing the energy and determining its work: it does not constitute the fuel of the engine, nor does it directly generate the power. Finance manipulates the patriotic forces which

> politicians, soldiers, philanthropists, and traders generate; the enthusiasm for expansion which issues from these sources, though strong and genuine, is irregular and blind; the financial interest has those qualities of concentration and clear-sighted calculation which are needed to set imperialism to work.[12]

Hobson's theory of imperialism was followed up mainly by German and Austrian Marxists, who tried to incorporate it into the framework of their ideology, for Hobson's analysis is fundamentally compatible with Marxism. It stresses the class orientation of the imperialist objectives; it points out the role of accumulation and monopolization of capital; and it regards underconsumption and/or overproduction at home as the basic cause of the expansionist policies.

Rudolph Hilferding of Austria was the first Marxist theoretician to build upon Hobson's analysis. In his book *Finance Capital*, which was written in 1905, Hilferding stresses the new forms of capitalist competition such as cartels and trusts and maintains that in this advanced stage capitalism requires the intervention of the state in order to continue its necessary expansion. He shows that the banks, particularly in Germany and the United States, had the leading role in controlling industrial capital. In the early period of imperialism economic objectives could be achieved by economic means, but finance capital could not override national boundaries without political and military support.

The monopoly capitalists in each nation-state, according to Hilferding, seek to bring new areas under their jurisdiction to safeguard capital investment, develop raw material production and guarantee markets for their outputs. It is due to the national development of capitalism and the national conflict of monopolies that "finance capital needs a strong state which recognizes finance capital's interests abroad and uses political power to exhort favorable treaties from smaller states, a state which can exert its influence all over the world in order to be able to turn the entire world into a sphere of investment. Finance capital finally needs a state which is strong enough to carry out a policy of expansion and to gather in new colonies.[13]

Hilferding concluded that finance capital cannot remain satisfied with the domination of the home market alone. The increasing monopolization of industry brought about by finance capital must result in overseas expansion. This means that colonies are no longer just for the export of consumption goods and the extraction of raw materials, but also for the export of finance capital. Nevertheless, Hilferding maintained that imperialism is a policy of capitalism and not a stage in its development. Like Hobson, he used his theory to argue for market expansion and income redistribution in England.

Karl Kautsky, a German Marxist, came to a similar conclusion in his analysis of imperialism. But he maintained that the exploitation of the world by internationally united finance capital may replace the rivalries of national finance capitals.

> What Marx said of capitalism can also be applied to imperialism: monopoly creates competition and competition monopoly. The frantic competition of giant firms, giant banks and multimillionaires obliged the great financial groups, who were absorbing the small ones to think up the notion of the cartel. In the same way, the result of the World War between the great imperialist powers may be a federation of the strongest, who renounce their arms race. Hence from the purely economic standpoint it is not impossible that capitalism may still live through another phase, the translation of cartellization into foreign policy: a phase of *ultra-imperialism*, which of course we must struggle against as energetically as we do against imperialism, but whose perils lie in another direction, not in that of the arms race and the threat to world peace.[14]

In his essay, *Imperialism: The Highest Stage of Capitalism*, V.I. Lenin argues that the most important consequence of the late 19th century imperialist expansion was the final partition of the globe, "...not in the sense that a new partition is impossible—on the contrary, new partitions are possible and inevitable—but in the sense that the colonial policy of the capitalist countries has completed the seizure of the unoccupied territories on our planet."[15] Lenin regards Hobson's *Imperialism* and Hilferding's *Finance Capital* as the most valuable contributions to the study of imperialism, but he rejects their theoretical perspective as "...Marxist opportunism" and their conclusions as "...bourgeois social reformism."[16]

For Lenin the term imperialism has a definite technical meaning. It refers to a special stage in the development of capitalism. He writes, "...if it were necessary to give the briefest possible definition of imperialism we should have to say that imperialism is the monopoly stage of capitalism."[17] The meaning of monopoly in this statement is more than literal—it connotes the passage from competitive capitalism to one in which trusts and cartels dominate the market. The expansionist drives of the advanced capitalist states are rooted in the irrepressible growth of monopoly and finance capital. The political and ideological forces which support such expansion are superstructural. At times nationalist and ideological spokesmen seem to control the process of expansion, but beneath the surface it is the economic imperatives of capitalism which play the dominant role. Thus, Lenin accepts the factual description of Hobson, but he maintains that there is an inevitable causal relationship between capitalism and imperialism. For Hobson, imperialism is a policy; for Lenin, it is a necessity.

Lenin emphasizes that the need for raw materials is a source of imperialism to a much greater degree than either liberal Hobson or Marxists Hilferding and Kautsky. He writes,

> The principal feature of modern capitalism is the domination of monopolist combines of the big capitalists. These monopolies are most firmly established when all the sources of raw materials are controlled by the one group. And we have seen with what zeal the international capitalist combines exert every effort to make it impossible for their rivals to compete with them; for example, by buying up mineral lands, oil fields, etc. Colonial possession alone gives complete guarantee of success to the monopolies against all the risks of the struggle with competitors, including the

> risk that the latter will defend themselves by means of a law establishing a state monopoly. The more capitalism is developed, the more the need for raw materials is felt, the more bitter competition becomes, the more feverishly the hunt for raw materials proceeds throughout the whole world, the more desperate becomes the struggle for the acquisition of colonies.[18]

Lenin rejects Kautsky's arguments concerning the development of ultra-imperialism and internationally united finance capital as reactionary and un-Marxist. He writes,

> The characteristic feature of imperialism is precisely that it strives to annex not only agricultural regions, but even highly industrialized regions (German appetite for Belgium; French appetite for Lorraine), because 1) the fact that the world is already divided up obliges those contemplating a new division to reach out for any kind of territory; and 2) because an essential feature of imperialism is the rivalry between a number of great powers in the striving for hegemony, i.e., for the conquest of territory, not so much directly for themselves as to weaken the adversary and undermine his hegemony. (Belgium is chiefly necessary to Germany as a base for operations against England; England needs Baghdad as a base for operations against Germany, etc.)[19]

Lenin also rejects Hobson's contention that surplus capital can be invested at home to raise the living standards of the masses.

> It goes without saying that if capitalism could develop agriculture, which today lags far behind industry everywhere, if it could raise the standard of living of the masses, who are everywhere still poverty-stricken and underfed, in spite of the amazing advance in technical knowledge, there could be no talk of a superabundance of capital. This 'argument' the petty-bourgeois critics of capitalism advance on every occasion.

> But if capitalism did these things it would not be capitalism; for uneven development and wretched conditions of the masses are fundamental and inevitable conditions and premises of this mode of production. As long as capitalism remains what it is, surplus capital will never be utilized for the purpose of raising the standard of living of the masses in a given country, for this would mean a decline in profits for the capitalists; it will be used for the purpose of increasing those profits by exporting capital abroad to the backward countries.[20]

Thus, for Lenin, imperialism is capitalism grown into a system of worldwide oppression and exploitation of the masses by a handful of rich and powerful states. These states choose to bribe the labor leaders and create a "labor aristocracy" in order to maintain their domination.

The central contention of the Leninist analysis is that capitalism is *inherently expansionist and breeds war*. The imperialist powers are bound to compete with one another; imperialism inevitably leads to militarism and war. Since imperialism can be ended only with the total destruction of capitalism as a system of production and distribution, the destruction of capitalism is the precondition for solving the problem of war. (The corollary of this is that there will be no war in a socialist world.) And those thinkers and policymakers who claim that the internecine and parasitic consequences of imperialism can be eliminated without eliminating capitalism are either short sighted or conscious deceivers of the masses.

Joseph A. Schumpeter is perhaps the most distinguished social thinker who set out to criticize both the liberal and Marxist theories of imperialism and provided an alternative socio-psychological explanation. Schumpeter maintains that "...imperialism is the objectless disposition on the part of the state to unlimited forcible expansion."[21] Since imperialist expansion is never satisfied by the fulfillment of a concrete interest, it cannot be explained by a concrete interest either. "Hence the tendency of such expansion to transcend all bounds and tangible limits."[22] Historical evidence shows that "...'objectless' tendencies toward forcible expansion, without definite, utilitarian limits—that is, non-rational and irrational, purely instinctual inclination toward war and conquest—play a very large role in the history of mankind. It may sound paradoxical, but numerous wars—perhaps the majority of all wars—have been waged without adequate 'reason'—not so much from the moral viewpoint as from that of reasoned and reasonable interest."[23]

According to Schumpeter, the psychological dispositions and social structures which lead to imperialist expansion and war once had their meaning and life-preserving function, but they no longer have any utility in the modern world.

> Imperialism thus is atavistic in character. It falls into that group of surviving features from earlier ages that play such an important part in every concrete social situation. In other words, it is an element that stems from the living conditions, not of the present, but of the past, or put in terms of the economic interpretation of history, from past rather than present relations of production.... It is from absolute autocracy that the present age has taken over what imperialist tendencies it displays.[24]

Capitalism has the potential to lead to large-scale production, but large-scale production does not have to lead to unlimited concentration. Trusts and cartels cannot pursue their monopolistic policies without protective tariffs; but "...protective tariffs do not automatically grow from the competitive system. They are the fruit of political action—a type of action that by no means reflects the objective interests of the majority of all those concerned."[25] Since a protective tariff is in the interest of the minority and does not result from the logic of capitalism as such, "...it is a basic fallacy to desribe imperialism as a necessary phase of capitalism, or even to speak of the development of capitalism into imperialism."[26]

In a purely capitalist world, according to Schumpeter, imperialist tendencies are bound to be regarded as distractions from the true task of life. The competitive capitalist system "...absorbs the full energies of most of the people at all economic levels.... There is much less energy to be vented in war and conquest than in any pre-capitalist society.... The point is that its people are likely to be essentially of an unwarlike disposition."[27] The development of capitalism, in other words, has been influenced by the needs and interests of the precapitalist social environment. Capitalism brought about many changes in the land and in the productive process, but it did not initially change the social structure and the political goals of the society. "This explains why the features and trends of autocracy—including imperialism—proved so resistant, why they exerted such a powerful influence on capitalist development, why the old export monopolism could live on and merge into the new."[28]

Schumpeter bases his analysis of imperialism on the performances of past empires, including the Egyptian, Frankish and Arabian. He is fundamentally interested in the question of why the capitalist classes governing modern nations act in an irrational and self-destructive fashion. He writes, "...there is but one way to an understanding: scrutiny of domestic class interests, the question of who stood to gain. [The ruling class] was always inclined to declare that the country was in danger *when it was really only class interests that were threatened.*"[29] This contention is identical with that of the Marxists. However, Schumpeter diverges from the Marxists by arguing that historical evidence has shown that irrational, instinctual urges towards war and conquest also play an important role in shaping history.

Schumpeter's contention that the state has interests different from the capitalist class is borne out by the U.S. experience.[30] However, as Richard Barnet points out, "...despite Schumpeter's prophecy and contrary to his advice, neither capitalists nor capitalist states have interpreted their real interests as avoiding 'such things as protective tariffs, cartels, monopoly prices, forced exports (dumping), an aggressive economic policy, an aggressive foreign policy generally....' It is almost as if the State Department had taken Schumpeter's list of evils to be avoided as its guide."[31]

One does not have to accept Schumpeter's notion of atavism in order to appreciate his arguments concerning the limitations of the economic explanation of imperialism. He clearly shows that economic theories of imperialism often exclude cultural and psychological factors that are as much a part of the system as economic factors.

Neither the Marxist nor the liberal theories of imperialism were able to anticipate the developments in the advanced capitalist countries and their relationship with the underdeveloped countries in the post-World War II period. In defense of Lenin, he did not regard his *Imperialism* as the last word on the subject. He wrote the tract in 1916 with the specific purpose of explaining the nature of the forces which had caused the war. His claims were modest and qualified. It was left to the latter day Leninists to transform his analysis into a dogma. Today the territorial empires of Europe are gone and the frontierless imperialism of the United States defies the Leninist model. Sixty years of convulsive history has drastically changed the character of the "parasitic and decaying capitalism" whose imminent demise Lenin expected.

The breakup of the European empires and the accession of their colonies to political independence after World War II dramatically changed the form of imperialist domination. Imperialism could no longer be identified with colonialism. Lenin rejected the possibility of any substantive increase in the consuming capacity of the general public under capitalism. However, in the post-World War II period, advanced capitalist societies have raised the living standard of their masses beyond anyone's expectations. Yet capitalism remains as exploitative and alienating as ever before.

Post-World War II developments in international politics and economics made their impact on the evolution of theories of imperialism. Included in this category are the works of such analysts as Baran and Sweezy, Samir Amin and Johan Galtung. The central explanation of the discrepancies in the Leninist theory of imperialism is advanced by Baran and Sweezy in *Monopoly Capital.* They maintain that the Soviet-inspired challenge to capitalism has led to the containment of inter-capitalist competition. Furthermore, they feel the multinational corporations have become so powerful that the new U.S. empire is run by the corporate managers who use the national governments as tools to pursue their corporate interests. And their objective continues to be

> monopolistic control over foreign sources of supply and over foreign markets, enabling them (the monopolists) to buy and sell on specially privileged terms, to shift orders from one subsidiary to another, to favour this country or that depending on which one has the most advantageous tax, labor and other policies—in a word they want to do business on their own terms and wherever they choose...with allies and clients not trading partners.[32]

According to Baran and Sweezy, this development in the evolution of capitalism is necessitated by autocentric accumulation, that is, accumulation without external expansion. Autocentric accumulation causes the rate of profit to fall at the center. In an attempt to solve this problem, capital moves to the periphery in search of a better return, but this response proves to be inadequate in absorbing the excess capital. Thus, state monopoly capitalism develops in order to organize the absorption of the surplus.

Monopoly Capital takes into account new facts relative to the way capitalism today attempts to overcome the permanent contradiction between the capacity to produce and the capacity to consume. Thus, the theory of monopoly capitalism demonstrates how the system can continue to function not by ending the "law of the increase of the surplus" but by finding the forms whereby this surplus can be absorbed. The theory also explains why the cycle of "the general cycle" was caused by the inability of the system to "plan" investment. Now, with the active assistance of the state, monopoly capitalism can engage in planning within certain limits. Thus, the cycle in its classical form is replaced by oscillations that are irregular and of smaller dimensions.

Samir Amin is the most well-known economic analyst of contemporary imperialism in the Third World. He maintains that the assistance provided by advanced capitalist countries does not contribute to the progress and independence of underdeveloped nations. Rather, the aid perpetuates the existing relationship of dominance and dependence between rich and poor countries.

Amin holds that the imperialist epoch falls into two periods: from 1880 to 1945, and from 1945 to the present. Until World War II the colonial system imposed classical forms upon the international division of labor. "The colonies provided the products of the *economie de traite* ('tropical' agricultural produce); European capital was invested in mining and in the tertiary sectors linked with this colonial exploitation (banking and trade, railways and ports, the public debt, etc.); the advanced centers supplied manufactured consumer goods."[33] In this period imperialism had an impoverishing effect on the periphery and led to a primary type of "blocked development."

According to Amin, the present period of imperialism is marked by three important structural changes: "1) the constitution of giant transnational firms...; 2) the impact of a technological revolution that transfers the center of gravity of the industries of the future toward new branches (atomic power, space research, electronics)...; and 3) the concentration of technological knowledge in these giant transnational firms."[34]

In this phase, the imperialist relationship between the center and periphery changes. For example, the monopolies can increase their rate of profit by technological domination instead of investing physical capital. Thus, "the return flow of profits from the periphery to the center is going to increase, and the underdeveloped countries are going to become sources of capital for the center."[35] Furthermore, technological domination has made it possible for "a new type of unequal international specialization to take shape."[36]

Johan Galtung is undoubtedly one of the most original analysts of imperialism in the contemporary world. He neither assumes nor rejects the primacy of economics in his general theory of imperialism. He writes,

> It is strongly felt that imperialism is a general structure that may be filled with very concrete economic, political, social, cultural, and communicative content—

> singly or in any combination. It may well be that at the present juncture in world history, in looking at international relations at large, an economic point of view would be the most fruitful in explaining what is going on. However, it is felt that there is a need for a broader theory of imperialism that also can come to grips with other phenomena, some of them very contemporary, some of them from the past, some of them to come in a possibly very near future.[37]

Furthermore, Galtung maintains that any analysis defining imperialism in terms of only two classes or groupings has fundamental shortcomings. The comfortable workers in rich countries cannot be placed in the same class as the miserable workers in poor countries simply because they are all called workers. The rich in different countries cannot be placed in a single class either. "The total conflict formation, hence, should be conceived of in terms of four classes or groups rather than in terms of two, and analytic schemes that purport to reflect the empirical reality of today should be flexible enough to accommodate some of the many variations found in the conflict constellations."[38]

Galtung believes that these complex contemporary circumstances limiting the value of using countries as units of analysis also demand a new approach to the study of imperialism. On the one hand the country as an analytical building block

> is too comprehensive, it gives an image of a country as a class-divided billiard ball, not sufficiently reflecting other internal differentiations.... On the other hand the image of the world as divided into countries does not reflect nonterritorial entities, such as some of the international organizations.[39]

Another problem to be taken under consideration is that "theories of imperialism have so far mainly been used to explain how basic inequities and inequalities are generated."[40] Galtung feels, however, that this is too narrow a scope in studying the reality of imperialism. He writes, "not only inequality, but also repression can often be traced to imperialistic relationships.

There is a strong center somewhere from which patterns emerge —thought patterns and cosmologies as well as social patterns and structures."[41]

Galtung's view is quite compatible with the theoretical theme of this book, namely that imperialism as a transnational system of privilege is a structure with multifaceted motivational sources, and it can only be understood within a structure-oriented perspective. Wicked people always influence the operation of the system, but a perspective based on wicked motives or goals cannot explain the reality of the imperialist structure.

Going Beneath and Beyond the Marxist and Liberal Theories

The emergence of the colonies as independent nation states, and the dramatic rise of the standard of living of the working class in the advanced capitalist countries have required the revision of the original Marxist theories in order to maintain their explanatory value in contemporary world politics. These neo-Marxist theories explain how imperialism in the guise of neocolonialism has been forced by colonial revolutions and domestic working class militance to develop new forms of exploitation in both the center and the periphery. In fact, the rise of the standard of living in the advanced countries and the growth of the middle class have been made possible in large part by the creation of a new international system of economic dependence. Neocolonialism is, on the one hand, a strategic concession to the revolt of the oppressed in the former colonies. On the other hand, it is a more systematic way of exploiting the Third World, which makes it possible to lessen the exploitation of certain sectors of the labor force in the advanced capitalist countries. Neo-Marxist theories are thus able to significantly advance our understanding of these changes in post-World War II U.S. imperialism.

But there are a number of more fundamental problems which the Marxist paradigm seems incapable of adequately explaining. These problems are perhaps best highlighted by the inability of Marxists to explain Soviet imperialism. According to Lenin, the destruction of capitalism will inevitably result in the demise of imperialism. But more than sixty years after the October Revolution the consolidation of the U.S.S.R. has not resulted in the lessening of Russian imperialism. On the contrary, the tentacles of the Soviet Union are reaching ever deeper into Africa, Central America, the Middle East and Southeast Asia. The existence of Soviet imperialism calls into question the whole Marxist paradigm; if capitalism can be eliminated without eliminating imperialism, then there must be other factors which contribute to imperialism other than capitalist economic factors.

The Marxist paradigm is flawed by its economic determinism. By assuming that the political sphere, the military, ideology, culture and all aspects of society are ultimately explainable by the economic structure of capitalism—by exploitation and class relations—Marxists have become blind to the multi-dimensionality of social processes and the centrality of human motivation and choice in understanding any socio-economic system. The "socialist" alternative as institutionalized in the Soviet Union suffers from moral bankruptcy.

There has not been a genuine social revolution in the Soviet Union because there has not been an expansion of freedom. The Soviet Union is a conservative police state. Its citizens have received limited security, but no freedom. Freedom in the Soviet Union is either a bourgeois mystification or a stage (true communism) which will eventually evolve once economic necessity has been overcome. Based on the economic determinism which underlies their policies and world outlook, the Soviet Communist Party justifies its dictatorship as necessary for building the material base upon which communist freedom can flourish. But freedom can never be an appendage to economic security. The separation of freedom from economic security, or regarding it as a by-product of economic development, is a rationalization for justifying the continued dominance of certain elites and the oppression of the vast majority of the population. Analogously, the continued oppression of women or of national minorities within the Soviet Union is tolerated because the economic basis for their liberation has not yet been achieved.

The primary concern of the Soviet leadership is not for the freedom of the Russian people, or for the freedom of the oppressed peoples in the underdeveloped countries, but for the perpetuation and expansion of their own political, economic, ideological and military power. Internationally, the Soviet Union could be genuinely revolutionary by challenging U.S. and Western imperialism. Instead, they functionally ally themselves with progressive and nationalist forces, not because they agree with their aims, but because they are necessary allies in their pursuit of global dominance. For instance, the Soviet alliance with the Palestinian movement has nothing to do with genuine support for Palestinian self-determination, but is only a strategy in the superpower struggle with the U.S. In fact, the Soviet Union originally supported Israel as a presumably progressive state in a sea of Arab reaction. Or to take another example, the Soviet Union opposed the Iranian nationalization of the British oil companies in 1951 for fear of losing its access to oil in northern Iran. But later in the oil crisis of the 1970s, the Soviet Union supported nationalization of Western oil companies as a way of opposing the U.S. Political and economic expediency determines the Soviet allies. In addition the Soviets purported support for liberation struggles in the underdeveloped countries to legitimize the domestic repression within the Soviet Union, much in the same way that the U.S. protection of the "Free World" is used to justify the arms buildup and domestic repression.

To be anti-imperialist is a moral choice. It is not just a question of the functional coincidence of material interests. To be anti-imperialist is to support oppressed peoples' struggles to be free, even if it is not in one's self-interest to do so.

Soviet domination, domestically or internationally, is justified by economic necessity, while freedom is seen as a secondary concern. It is in this light that the economic determinism of Marxist theories of imperialism is suspect for failing to comprehend the noneconomic sources of power and the many ways in which domination is perpetuated regardless of the economic structure. Just as bourgeois ideology mystifies capitalist exploitation, Marxist ideology tends to obscure noneconomic forms of oppression in "socialist" countries.

More specifically, the economic determinism of Marxist theories results in a failure to understand that the political, military and ideological dimensions of imperialism are not superstructural reflections of economic factors, but rather, that each has a specific dynamism of its own. For instance, the state bureaucracy, whether in advanced or underdeveloped countries, has its own specific interests and constantly seeks to perpetuate itself. At times the interests of the state may coincide with the interests of the dominant classes in a society, but at other times they may be in conflict. The state is not simply a tool of the ruling class, nor a structure determined by the economy, nor simply an arena for class struggle. The state has a life of its own. The livelihood of a large percentage of the population, as well as the dominant political elite, is dependent on the continued growth and expansion of the state sector.

The Pentagon, as the most visible expression of the military in the U.S., has its own expansionist aims which are, as often as not, in conflict with the interests of U.S. multinational corporations. At times there may be a functional convergence of interests among the military, the arms producers and broad sectors of the capitalist class. At other times the military's pursuit of its own development directly conflicts with aims of the government and the multinational corporations, thwarting attempts to arrange international economic, political and military coordination and agreements. The fight over the Panama Canal may be understood in this light.

Perhaps more noticeably than its failure to understand the power of either the state or the military, the economic determinism of Marxist theories of imperialism fails to understand that nationalism is a profound expression of the need of people to identify with a larger group. In the last couple of hundred years the nation has become this group. While it is true that nationalism takes the form of defensive and oppositional movements in its attempts to resist capitalist and imperialist exploitation, it can also be a positive force through which the self-identity of a people is created and maintained. History, tradition, culture, language, environmental and geographic factors combine to determine national identity. The need for national self-determination is not simply a front for opposing imperialism, or furthering socialism. It is the genuine and indispensable need of individuals in a nation to express their consciousness of their historical identity and to create a nation-state in accordance with their understanding. This need of the people may coincide with widely divergent class interests, but in no way can it be reduced to class interests. The Iranian revolution exemplifies beyond doubt the power and desire of an oppressed people to be free as a nation.

These weaknesses of the Marxist theories of imperialism begin to reveal the failure of economic determinism to understand the nature of being human. If the real concern of revolutionaries is for the liberation of all peoples, then human development must be at the center of our theories and strategies for revolutionary change. For human choice, the ability of human beings, whether as classes, nations, races, or genders, to self-consciously determine their futures constitutes their specific distinctiveness as a species. If this focus is maintained then it becomes impossible to understand human development as determined solely by material necessity. Any form of reductionism must fail to comprehend the human reality. The ability to reason and to decide constitutes our uniqueness as a species—our irreducibility. The incredible diversity of human societies testifies to the ever varied ways in which people have sought to shape their societies. Marx understood that people create the social institutions which, in turn, set the context in which subsequent choices are made. Thus, while human choices are always made in specific historical conditions, they are nonetheless choices—self-conscious choices made between a number of different options—not predetermined.

While the ability to choose constitutes our uniqueness as human beings, our need to identify with and to be recognized by each other—to experience unity—constitutes our commonality. The compassion and concern that motivates us to fight for the self-determination of all peoples springs from the realization of our common identity. Moreover, the ability of all peoples to be self-determining depends on their realization that the freedom depends on the freedom of all—that ultimately individual freedom depends on the ability of all peoples to collectively determine the future of humanity. It is from this perspective that opposition to U.S. imperialism is a profoundly moral decision.

Chapter 1 Footnotes

1. Harrison M. Wright, ed., *The New Imperialism: Analysis of Late Nineteenth Century Expansion* (Boston: D.C. Heath and Co., 1961), pp. vii-viii.
2. J.A. Hobson, *Imperialism: A Study* (London: Allen and Unwin, 1902), p. 106.
3. Ibid.
4. Ibid., p. 12.
5. Ibid., p. 14.
6. Ibid., p. 20.
7. Ibid., p. 21.
8. Ibid.
9. Ibid., p. 25.
10. Ibid., p. 30.
11. Ibid., p. 37.
12. Ibid., p. 63.
13. Ibid., p. 49.
14. Ibid., p. 52.
15. V.I. Lenin, *Imperialism: The Highest Stage of Capitalism* (New York: International Publishers), p. 76.
16. Ibid., p. 15.
17. Ibid., p. 88.
18. Ibid., p. 82.

19. Ibid., pp. 91-92.
20. Ibid., pp. 62-63.
21. Joseph Schumpeter, *Imperialism and Social Classes* (New York: Augustus M. Kelley, Inc., 1951), p. 5.
22. Ibid., p. 14.
23. Ibid., p. 23.
24. Ibid., p. 35.
25. Ibid., p. 40.
26. Ibid., p. 51.
27. Ibid., p. 70.
28. Ibid., p. 83.
29. Ibid., p. 53.
30. Richard Barnet, *Roots of War* (Baltimore: Penguin Books, 1972), pp. 176-205. Also, Franz Schurmann, *The Logic of World Power* (New York: Pantheon Books, 1974), pp. 8-17.
31. Barnet, *Roots of War*, p. 214.
32. Paul Baran and Paul M. Sweezy, *Monopoly Capital* (New York: Monthly Review Press, 1966), p. 201.
33. Samir Amin, *Unequal Development* (New York: Monthly Review Press, 1976), p. 188.
34. Ibid., p. 189.
35. Ibid., p. 190.
36. Ibid.
37. Johan Galtung, *The True Worlds: A Transnational Perspective* (New York: The Free Press, 1980), p. 108.
38. Ibid., p. 111.
39. Ibid.
40. Ibid.
41. Ibid., p. 112.

CHAPTER 2

U.S. IMPERIALISM: A TRANSNATIONAL SYSTEM OF PRIVILEGE

The purpose of this chapter is to develop a conceptual framework for analyzing the evolving character of U.S. imperialism in contemporary international politics. Neither the Marxist theories of neocolonialism nor the non-Marxist views that define imperialism as a relationship of domination/subordination between two nations provide an adequate model for describing the transnational realities of the present day imperialist relations.

Since the term imperialism came into popular use, its connotations have changed several times. The connotations of words which refer to dynamic realities change as the context and specific characteristics of the reality to which they refer change. The word imperialism has always been used to describe the dynamic reality of a system of privilege in the relations among nations. A system of privilege involves exploitation, dependence and inequity.[1]

An imperialist system does not have to be formally constituted in order to be recognized as such. It is the actual exercise of its power, the nature of its objectives and the practical consequences of its policies that define its reality. It does not particularly matter what the imperialist policymakers call their activities in the official proclamations. The British called their expansion into Africa and Asia "the white man's burden"; the French described it as their "civilizing mission"; the Soviet Union justifies its domination of Eastern Europe in the name of international "socialist solidarity"; and the U.S. defends its global counter-revolutionary activities in the name of "human rights."

The issue is not sincerity. What people think they are doing matters less than what they are actually doing. This does not mean that the thoughts, motivations and intentions of policymakers are not important in understanding their actions. When it comes to the question of *why* a system of privilege exists, then a comprehension of the motives, intentions, values and thoughts of the dominant and the dominated is indispensable. But to determine whether or not imperialism, in fact, exists, one must focus on the conditions and relationships that constitute a system of privilege, namely, inequity, dependence and exploitation.

Inequity means whatever inequality there may be in a society or in an exchange that is structural, that is to say, the logical outcome of the established norms and patterns. Equality presupposes similarity in needs, while "equity is a rule against exploitation; it rules out interaction relations that lead to uneven external and internal benefits."[2]

Dependence means that a need is generated in the exploited society that can be satisfied only by the imperialist power. This is a need of the elites, not the masses, but it is interpreted as a need of the society as a whole. As Galtung puts it,

> dependency is essentially a power relation: it means that what happens in the periphery is a consequence of causes located in the center. Thus, it gives broader scope to "power" than is usually given in actor-oriented analysis where the "cause" referred to has to

be somebody's *intent* to exercise power; it also takes in the type of power that is built into a structure.[3]

Exploitation means that something is expropriated from the exploited and appropriated by the exploiter; its meaning should include what goes on within the group of actors on each side of the relation. Thus, exploitation "should not be interpreted only in terms of bilateral relations between exploiter and exploited,...but as patterns of relations wherein after some time the total system proves to be much more beneficial for some components of the network than for others."[4]

A Transnational System of Privilege

Since the establishment of national self-determination in the former colonies, imperialism as a system of privilege has developed a transnational character. The term transnational is used here to describe those activities in world politics and economics which result from a congruence of interests between two or more nation-states. Such congruence of interests between states does not necessarily represent the existence of imperialistic relations, but when it does the resulting coalition constitutes a transnational system of privilege.

The interdependency of this transnational system of development does not change the inequity between the states. For example, in spite of complex interdependencies between the United States and the Shah of Iran, the relationship between them was highly inequitable because the ability of the Shah to change or modify the interdependency was far more limited than that of the United States. Inequity is an indispensable condition of imperialism.

Conventional analysts of world politics view the nation-states as the only actors in the international system and the pursuit of national interests and/or ideology as the core of their interplay, Chiefs of state, soldiers and diplomats—force or the threat of force—are the principal agents acting within the system; and the ability or willingness to compromise is the means by which war can be avoided in the unending struggle for power and privilege. The requirement of domestic order and stability is perceived as a motive in the formulation of foreign policy objectives and strategies, but it is not analyzed as a principal force in the interplay of the states.[5] This approach to the study of international relations could make sense if there were no actual domestic challenge to the power of the state and the socio-economic structure it represents.

But we live in a revolutionary age, a period in which many states are threatened by internal political elements that reject the foundation of their societies as unfair and illegitimate. In such situations the requirement of domestic order and stability can create a congruence of interests between two or more states overshadowing their competitive relations as independent states.

It is due to the development of such a situation that imperialist policies and actions today increasingly subordinate the interests of the general public to the interests of the ruling elites in both dominant and dominated societies. The key concept is subordination, whether direct or indirect. The ruling elites of the subordinated countries are the junior partners of the elites in the dominant countries. In some cases such as Iran, Brazil, Indonesia and the Philippines, the junior partners join in forming a sub-imperialist system. At times, nationalism and conflict of interests create tension and distrust between the senior and the junior partners, the imperialists and the sub-imperialists. The necessity of the partnership, however, is not questioned because it is a response to the revolutionary challenge to the structure of privilege in the subordinated societies. Washington feels as much threatened by this challenge to the status quo in the pro-Western Third World countries as the elites of these societies, who have to confront the revolutionaries at home.

Contemporary imperialism, therefore, does not have to involve impairment of national sovereignty. However, this does not change the reality of imperialism as a system of privilege. Transnationalism represents the ability of the privileged few in two or more nation-states to join forces across national boundaries and together confront the revolutionary challenge from below in the subordinated society. At the same time, this transnational system of privilege allows the dominant countries to pacify the domestic opposition by making possible a higher standard of living and providing the benefits of welfare capitalism.

Until recent decades the ruling elites in the official or unofficial colonies of Africa, Asia and Latin America did not need the assistance of colonial or imperialist powers in order to maintain their privileged position. In fact, in many cases the traditional rulers attempted to resist the Western penetration of their societies not only for political but also for cultural and ideological reasons. Until the outbreak of World War II, the cultural and ideological orientation of the typical ruling class in an underdeveloped country was not too different from that of the country's general population.[6]

To be sure, peasant life in the class-ridden underdeveloped countries was, and is, nasty, brutish and short. But the landed gentry or its equivalent had constant contact with the exploited peasants. They all identified with the same religious symbols and justified their actions and intentions in similar fashion. The mode of transportation and communication used by the owners of land and capital was not a mystery to the peasants. Privileged children visited the village regularly and their education and attitudes were familiar to the villagers.

Today the situation is completely changed. Peasants are still living under the same conditions or have moved to urban ghettos, but the owners or controllers of the means of production have adopted a cultural and ideological orientation that is a mystery to the general population. The privileged few, whether they belong to the entrepreneurial, bureaucratic or military sector of the ruling elite, have little socio-cultural contact with the exploited many. In terms of their concrete aspirations and ambitions, they identify with the West to the point of being alienated from their own roots. Their children are educated in the West and their lifestyles, attitudes, and values mystify the general public in their native lands.

Thus, as the economic gap between the privileged few and the wretched many increases, so does the cultural gap. The enclaves of wealth and power in countries like Egypt, Pakistan, Brazil, Indonesia and the Philippines are also enclaves of imported cultures and lifestyles. The presence of multinational corporations in such sub-imperialist countries benefits and strengthens these enclaves of wealth and power in the sea of misery. Of course, the national elites who control the political and economic institutions of the country have their disagreements with the managers of the multinational corporations. But the disagreements, when they do arise, usually relate to tactics of operation and to the share of profits the native elites receive.

The native elites, who have control over the means of production, consumption, and compulsion, may or may not be an autonomous social force. The intensity of their nationalism could vary from one country to another. The degree of their dependence on or interdependence with the industrialized countries cannot be determined a priori. These are issues which need to be investigated on a case by case basis.

What is clear in the present situation of international relations is the growing congruence of interests between the foreign policy elites in the industrialized world, particularly the United States, and the ruling elites of the class-ridden societies in the underdeveloped world. In confronting the revolutionary demands from below, these elites and their counterparts in the developed world have become interested in "revolution from above." The coalition of elites across national boundaries perceives economic development in the poor nations to be a necessity, not only as a means of expanding markets for Western products, but also as a means of enlarging the small middle class in the underdeveloped countries and as a way of legitimizing the rule of the privileged few. This kind of economic development has nothing to do with justice or equity because the distribution of accumulated wealth takes place in the context of the existing class structure. In countries such as Iran, South Korea and Brazil economic development has intensified class differences and the maldistribution of wealth and income.

Thus as transnational coalitions develop, the role of the state in managing the life of the nation expands. As the interests of various states converge in the need to confront revolutionary challenges in the class-ridden underdeveloped countries, new issues enter the realm of interstate relations and domestic politics becomes internationalized. The consequences of these developments go far beyond the traditional questions involved in international politics and economics. In this age of revolutionary demand for equality, global standardization of elites' cultural values, worldwide dissemination of information and communications networks and the massive spread of sophisticated weapons and military technology, imperialism as a model for analyzing international relations must take into account the development of transnational interests and coalitions.

Four Dimensions of Imperialism

As we saw in the first chapter, Marxist theories of neocolonialism, while providing a useful framework for understanding the economic dimension of imperialism, were seriously flawed by their assumption that all other factors could be explained in terms of Marxist economic categories. The sources of transnational imperialism are more complex. They can be divided into four principal dimensions: the economic dimension, the political dimension, the military dimension and the ideological dimension. The dynamics of this system include, on the one hand, the activities taking place within each dimension and, on the other hand, the processes that connect the principal dimensions to one another. In this section we will incorporate into our understanding of transnational imperialism a multidimensional analysis which will explain the four principal sources of international domination.

The economic dimension encompasses the ways in which the imperialist system shapes the modes of production in both the dominant and subordinated countries so as to reinforce control of the former over the latter. The political dimension analyzes the power relationships within and between the nation states in the imperialist system. The military dimension analyzes the threat and use of force to assure the expansion of the military sector and the security of the dominant and subordinated countries. The ideological dimension entails the justifications and rationalizations of imperialism which become a material force and constitute the basis of the cultural hegemony of the dominant country. These four aspects of imperialism are called dimensions here to emphasize that while each is conceptually distinct and constitutes a specific form of imperialist domination, in reality these four dimensions are interwined and mutually reinforcing in the ever changing dynamic processes of transnational imperialism. The bases of these four forms of domination are the decisions and action of human beings either to perpetuate, or to tolerate, or to destroy imperialist domination.

The Economic Dimension

It is of the very essence of capitalism to expand. Growth is the law of capitalism. Competition within and between industries and nations, the need to control the international labor force and to have the size and power to influence the dominant and subordinate nation-states, forces capitalist firms to continually expand to gain as much profit and power as possible. As corporations get bigger they tend to diversify both industrially and geographically. Today the value of the foreign subsidiaries and branches of U.S.-based corporations is more than $100 billion. Their sales have been rising faster than the domestic sales of U.S. corporations, and their earnings are equivalent to about 25 percent of the net profits of the U.S. corporations. While local capitalists or governments in the underdeveloped countries retain a significant segment of their country's economy, it has been predicted that in another 20 years 500-600 corporations will control most of the capitalist world's business. One observer has estimated that by the end of this century "a regime of 300 or 400 multinational corporations will control 50 percent to 70 percent of the world industrial output."[7] Of course, such estimates are based on the assumption that the revolutionary challenge to capitalism in the Third World will not succeed. Few, if any, of these corporations will be headquartered in the poor countries, but all will have subsidiaries in them involving junior partnership of the local elites.

There is no question that the presence of multinational corporations in a capitalist-oriented poor country is beneficial to the elites who control the economic and political institutions of their country. This is not to say that the local elites have no disagreement with the corporate executives. Far from it. The privileged elites in the poor countries are involved in constant bargaining and disagreement with the corporate representatives. But such bargaining or disagreement does not involve the question of whether the multinationals should operate in the countries. In other words, the elites of the class-ridden societies of Africa, Asia and Latin America do not question the general strategy of capitalist development; their questions and concerns, when they arise at all, relate to tactics and their share of the profits.

Unlike extractive investment, which operates as an "enclave" unconcerned with the growth of the local economy, manufacturing investment has a direct stake in the growth of the local market. The goods that manufacturing investment produces symbolize a way of life. The natives of the host country are to be persuaded to consume these goods. Thus, by introducing its wares and convincing people to buy them, the manufacturing investment participates in the shaping of the local culture. The transfer of ideas and tasks has a greater impact on the general population than the transfer of capital, although such impact cannot be comprehended or measured by quantitative economic models. Official Washington has to convince the local citizens that their interests are being served by the local elite policymakers. This objective can be achieved only if the state is able to increase both its own power and the economic privileges of the various segments of the society.

The majority of multinational corporations are U.S. corporations with production and distribution facilities located around the globe. Together with international finance capital, (e.g., Chase Manhattan) multinational corporations act as the primary agents of neocolonial domination by structuring the economies of the underdeveloped countries to fit the needs of the multinational corporations. The multinationals, in defense of their operations, often point to the increase in aggregate income which results from their operations. The national elites are the most unlikely candidates to question the appalling maldistribution of this growing aggregate income because they, constituting a tiny segment of the population, are its principal beneficiaries.

Furthermore, the multinational corporations are not only producers of goods but also transmitters of ideas and values from the advanced capitalist world to the poor countries. Thus, Marx's notion that "the ideas of the ruling class are in every epoch the ruling ideas" becomes a transnational reality. "The class which has the means of material production at its disposal, has control at the same time over the means of mental production, so that thereby, generally speaking, the ideas of those who lack the means of mental production are subject to it."[8]

In their book, *Global Reach*, Richard Barnet and Ronald Muller describe the leading executives of multinational corporations as "world managers."[9] These "world managers" need the active participation of the native elites in the poor nations in order to implement their corporate plans; the local elites need the resources of the multinationals in order to pursue their capitalist strategy for development. Richard Sklar has argued that this complex interdependency has led to,

> the formation of a transnational class comprising at its core those who manage multinational corporations. To substantiate this thesis, it would be necessary to show that the members of any such presumed class tend to think and act as a collective entity. Social classes are sustained and strengthened by many different generators of vitality. A transnational ruling class would be especially difficult to overthrow inasmuch as its power would be fortified by the appropriation of diverse resources in many countries. Its significance as a power group might transcend the conception of imperialism.[10]

Thus, corporate internationalism and the revolutionary threat to the class structure of underdeveloped countries have led to the functional coalescence of dominant classes across national boundaries. And the beneficiaries of this transnational coalition have even more in common than their opposition to revolution.

The ostentatious life style of the elites in the underdeveloped countries predates the arrival of multinational corporations or the congruence of transnational interests. But in recent decades this ostentatious life style has been divorced from its native roots. The rapid growth of international finance, movement of goods and services, travel and communication have led to a global standardization of values, goals and aspirations among the elites. Since the technology and the ideology involved in this dramatic phenomenon are products of organic socio-economic growth in the West, the standardization of values, goals and aspirations among the dominant elements in the transnational system of privilege has added a new dimension of cultural domination to the evolving character of imperialism in the contemporary world. Today even the liberal education, manners, style of dress, fads and consumptive norms of the elites in subordinated countries are similar to those of their counterparts in the advanced industrial world.

The U.S., as the chief imperialist power of our time, often justifies its support of the privileged elites in underdeveloped countries in the name of stability, which is regarded as the prerequisite for economic development. Since World War II, United States officials have conceived of development as a historical process by which societies have evolved from the primitive communities of the past to the industrial states of today. The term underdeveloped, therefore, is used to distinguish those societies which have fallen behind the countries whose quantitative progress remains uninterrupted.

Implicit in this view of underdevelopment is the equation of economic growth with qualitative advancement of the sociopolitical structures. This ethnocentric equation of aggregate/quantitative development with cultural/ideological advancement has been accepted by the elites in the subordinated countries.

Thus, the dominant elements in the transnational system of privilege define underdevelopment as traditionalism, low per capita income, widespread illiteracy, lack of political integration, a comparatively low degree of urbanization and industrialization, lack of institutional continuity, lack of national unity, particularism, functional diffuseness, and so on. This characterization may be useful as a first step in describing the conditions of some underdeveloped societies. But if the above variables are analyzed without inclusion of the class structure and imperialism, the result will be distorted both as an analytical tool and as a description of reality.

A meaningful conception of underdevelopment must include the recognition that class rule and imperialism are both the beneficiaries and the perpetuators of underdevelopment. Development requires structural change in both economic and socio-political institutions of the society. While economic growth can be defined as a steady accumulation of wealth and expansion of income, the process of development requires as a precondition the existence of a social structure in which wealth and income can be more equitably distributed. The absence of this precondition in the dominated societies of the transnational system of privilege makes the initial step of the development process an act of revolutionary liberation, which includes the destruction of the traditional ruling class.

This essential and recurring feature of the developmental process is antagonistic to both the short-run and the long-run objectives of United States imperialism. In the short-run national liberation movements will not side with the United States in its ideological rivalry with the Soviet Union, nor will they favor the continuation of exploitative international trade and investment policies. They will not allow multinational corporations to abuse their native resources or turn their countries into a market for U.S. surplus goods. In the long run, successful revolutionary governments might restructure their societies in ways that weaken the world capitalist order. They might give material support to other revolutionary movements in the underdeveloped countries and through the successful use of noncapitalist methods of development become a source of inspiration for other subordinated societies.

The Political Dimension

Politics is the domain where competition for power occurs as well as the domain where rationalizations for public policy and justification for the use of force are openly asserted. In these rationalizations politicians always claim to be the servants of society and never appear as its masters. However, political power is an end in itself as well as a means to achieve moral and material ends, and thus constitutes an independent source of imperialism. There is, historically speaking, a relationship between the concentration of power in the nation-state system and the urge to dominate other nations. This urge manifests itself in the relations among nations regardless of the value orientation of their economic order. Furthermore, it is a fact of history that not all actions taken by individual rulers or factions for the purpose of perpetuating or expanding their own power are the logical derivatives of institutional settings, ideology or objective material conditions, although they are always connected.

The political dimension of imperialist policy formation relates to the struggle for power and influence within and between states. In open societies political competition is a public affair and valued as a necessary activity, while in closed societies political competition is a mystified and hidden activity. The citizens of open societies play a significant role in the political arena through their votes, while their counterparts in closed societies have no such role to play. Elections, however, do not necessarily mean that there is genuine public participation in political affairs or that there is a higher degree of identification/satisfaction with the state on the part of the citizens. Of course, taking popular preferences into consideration does not automatically mean that they will be respected or satisfied. In the case of imperialist powers it often means manipulating and deceiving the public.

There is no reason to believe that the American people wanted their country to be militarily involved in Vietnam. There was no popular mandate. But three presidents acted without this mandate and engaged United States troops in the most irrational war of this century. John F. Kennedy's aide Kenneth O'Donnel has written that two months before his assassination President Kennedy expressed the view that U.S. troops in Vietnam had to be withdrawn but that it could not be done until after his re-election. The president was afraid of right wing criticism and its possible negative impact on his re-election efforts. What if Kennedy had not been afraid of right wing critics and had actually extricated the United States from the Indochina war? Needless to say, the history of the United States as well as the course of international politics over the past fifteen years would have been very different. There is no question that Cold War considerations within the domestic political scene played a significant role in determining the character and length of U.S. military involvement in Vietnam.

After the 1967 Middle East war a high ranking State Department official tried to explain to President Lyndon Johnson that there were actually two sides to the Arab-Israeli conflict. The president replied, "How many Arab voters are there in Chicago and how much have they contributed to my campaign?" There is little doubt that Jewish voters in the United States have been disproportionately influential in shaping U.S. policies toward the Arab Middle East. President Johnson's response to the suggestion that there were actually two sides to the Arab-Israeli conflict was not even consistent with the views of his own State Department, but it was certainly in harmony with his renomination and re-election strategy. The president's remark was also consistent with the attitudes of his predecessors toward the Middle East dilemma.

A significant characteristic of the political sources of imperialism is that they are often based on short-term and factional considerations. Thus, they are not always rational or consistent with the long-term objectives of the state. Modern state bureaucracies are plagued with the kind of reactive and self-serving behavior which has more to do with their internal competition than with national policy.

An important factor which has enhanced the role of the political dimension in contemporary imperialism is the financial independence of the state. In the 19th century the imperialist states were dependent on funds from the private capital market for financing discretionary expansionist undertakings and thus their economic policies had to enable the colonies to meet their private debt service. Today, due to their financial independence, the imperialist states can not only allow more flexible fiscal policies but can also forgo economic benefits in order to keep a particular government or socio-political order in power.

The significance of this development lies in the ability of the contemporary imperialist state to support its political or ideological objectives and to export capital without a quid pro quo. Military aid, grants and low cost loans extended to underdeveloped countries by AID are the main examples of this mode of operation.

Social imperialism, the term chosen by the Chinese to describe Soviet imperialism, has a very important meaning because it connotes the efforts of a superpower to reproduce its own social configuration elsewhere. Whether or not this is done for material gain does not change its imperialistic character. Social imperialism means a superpower would be willing to forego economic benefits, long-term as well as short-term, in order to control a society or impose a particular structure on it.

The Military Dimension

Imperialism is a system of power to which the vast majority of people in the United States have, however reluctantly, submitted. U.S. imperialism, therefore, cannot be examined only with regard to moral concerns, but also in the context of its responsiveness to the real requirements of the existing socioeconomic system.

The economics and politics of imperialism entangle the nation at large in a security-oriented alliance with the government. It seems to be in the nature of imperialism to fear everything that is not subject to its influence. This fear, which has always been present in the imperialist countries, has a functional value for the state. Without continuing insecurity and fear in the public, imperialism as a form of government cannot be maintained and rationalized. Imperial powers have always appealed to the basest instincts of their people while claiming to be the fountainhead of universal welfare.

Keynes advocated public works projects as a way to fight recession. After the second world war this tactic was replaced by parasitic military spending. Fear of communism and the dynamic of the post-war global expansion made the defense budget politically acceptable as the principal stimulator of the economy. The business community welcomed defense spending because military appropriations never encountered any difficulty in Congress. The labor unions regarded it as a source of job security, and the general public accepted wasteful defense expenditures in the name of national security.

The Kennedy Administration rejected Eisenhower's "massive retaliation" strategy and adopted the more complicated and politically ambitious strategy of "flexible response." This strategy meant a major increase in the apparatus of the Pentagon and an even more extensive increase in the United States' political involvement in the internal affairs of underdeveloped countries. The specific policies of "flexible response" were designed to fight a multi-dimensional war on the military, social and political levels, with the goal of destroying revolutionary movements in the underdeveloped world. "So that, while the nuclear stalemate with Soviet Russia has resulted in probable peace at the highest technological level for our time, the enormous potential for smaller international conflicts, civil war and guerrilla wars now compels the United States to maintain an equally enormous military establishment on a permanent basis in order to deal with the countless brush fires that are sure to flare up repeatedly over a great part of the world."[11] Thus, the United States became the policeman of the non-Communist world and found itself saddled with an unprecedented military establishment.

The United States has never had a military cult intense enough to glorify war. Absence of a military cult in U.S. history is one of the unique aspects of U.S. imperialism. The Continental Congress stated in 1787, "Standing armies in time of peace are inconsistent with principles of republican governments, dangerous to the liberties of a free people and generally converted into a destructive engine for establishing despotism." At the turn of the century some writers made a few statements in praise of violent conflict for its own sake, but they had little influence on public opinion. As Hofstadter writes, even "such outbursts as [Theodore] Roosevelt's 'Strenuous Life' speech were rare; and it was also rare for a U.S. writer to extol war for its effects upon the race, although Rear Admiral Stephen B. Luce, one of Mahans' patrons, once declared that 'strife in one form or another in the organic world seems to be the law of existence.'"[12] In fact, the U.S. is, in many ways, one of the least militaristic societies in the world. The post-World War II imperialist expansion, however, dealt a severe blow to this view of the military in U.S. society.

Seymour Melman has shown in his empirical studies that capitalist profit motive does not adequately explain the motivation of U.S. imperialist policies.

> The government of the United States now includes a self-expanding war machine that uses military power for diverse political operations and is based upon an industrial management that has priority claims to virtually unlimited capital funds from the federal budget. ...To the older pattern of exploitative imperialism abroad, there is now added an institutional network that is parasitic at home.[13]

The requirements of running an empire often defy personal preferences, including those of the emperor himself. Years after leaving office, "President Truman was to lament the extension of the CIA's functions from intelligence-gathering to actual armed operations and claimed that 'the last thing we needed was for the CIA to be seized upon as something akin to a subverting influence in the affairs of other people.' But, for all that, it was President Truman himself who, in 1951, established the Plans Division which was put in charge of the CIA's special operations."[14]

The Central Intelligence Agency has been an effective tool of United States imperialism since World War II. This enormous apparatus has substantially reduced the power of professional diplomats. Allen W. Dulles, the first director of the CIA, once observed that "the National Security Act of 1947 has given Intelligence a more influential position in our government than intelligence enjoys in other governments in the world."[15]

Whatever choices may have been made in the 1890s or 1910s or 1940s, once they were made they developed their own imperatives and influenced the consciousness of all those involved. Imperialist actions create certain economic, political and ideological conditions by which the position of the privileged is perpetuated. Thus, the interests of the underprivileged develop in opposition to those of the privileged.

Economics is not the only cause of militarism and war. For example, the *Pentagon Papers* demonstrates that it was not capitalism per se that motivated the United States to get involved in the Indochina war.[16] Rather, it was U.S. power, which happened to have a capitalist economic base, that acted aggressively in pursuit of its perceived benefits. Four successive administrations, from Eisenhower to Nixon, believed it important for strategic and ideological reasons to keep South Vietnam out of communist hands, even though the United States had no direct economic interest in Southeast Asia.[17]

The Leninist contention that the abolition of war can come only after the destruction of the capitalist system everywhere conflicts with the fact that exploitation, territorial expansion and war existed long before modern capitalism. If private ownership of the means of production is the only cause of war and conflict, then how does one explain the war between the People's Republic of China and the People's Republic of Vietnam? How does one explain the invasion of "socialist" Czechoslovakia by the "socialist" Soviet Union?

Given the economic, strategic and ideological objectives of U.S. foreign policy, it is quite logical that United States policymakers are determined to strengthen the military and political institutions of their junior partners in the transnational system of privilege, aiding in their confrontation with the revolutionary challenge. The theoretical justification for this policy goes back to the post-World War II period. Dean Acheson, John Foster Dulles, Walt Rostow, Henry Kissinger and Zbigniew Brzezinski all maintained that the underdeveloped countries are going through the stage of development in which the traditional society is transformed into a modern political community.

During this turbulent transformation the masses are vulnerable to revolutionary propaganda and they have to be protected from their own feelings and tendencies. The United States must give the national privileged elites military, political and economic support against the revolutionaries but should try to avoid overt military action if at all possible. These same people thought Vietnam was a mistake. Once the transitional stage of instability is ended by economic growth and proper socialization of the masses, there will no longer be any need for U.S. involvement in the internal affairs of the underdeveloped countries.[18]

It is quite logical that the United States has become a generous exporter of arms and repressive technology to the subordinated countries, particularly the sub-imperialists. United States military sales to the underdeveloped countries since 1970 amount to $41 billion, plus $13 billion in credit sales and $7 billion in commercial sales. United States military assistance in grants and credits to underdeveloped countries between 1946 and 1976 amounted to $71 billion. U.S. assistance to the police forces of underdeveloped countries from 1961-1978 amounted to $322 million.[19] Besides bringing revenue to the arms industry, such a vast transfer of arms and repression technology is supposed to enable the junior partners in the transnational system of privilege to protect themselves against revolutionary movements.

While President Carter was speaking of his "undeviating commitment" to human rights, some of the most insidious torturers of the world were continuing to receive weapons, repression technology and intelligence training and advice from the United States. Such police states as Argentina, Brazil, Chile, Indonesia, the Philippines, South Korea, Thailand and Uruguay have been among the principal recipients of U.S. weapons and repression technology.[20]

However, the development of nuclear weapons has dramatically changed the historic link between imperialism and war. It was Karl Kautsky who first theorized about "ultra-imperialism" or peaceful imperialist rivalry as an alternative to Lenin's prediction of the inevitability of war between imperialist states. Kautsky's theory turned out to be wishful thinking, but the destruction of Hiroshima and Nagasaki created a situation in which peaceful imperialist rivalry became a necessity. As Frantz Schurmann writes,

> Nuclear policy was the weapon with which America built its empire, for no other policy so clearly stated

> America's global intentions with ramifications for everything else. Nuclear policy was pure policy in that its operational consequences were nil or limited to building and deploying weapons which, of course, could not be used. The operational ramifications came in other areas—military, political, economic, and even cultural.[21]

Richard Barnet maintains that the Vietnam War forced the managers of the U.S. corporate economy to ask themselves seriously for the first time whether or not territorial control and political influence abroad are worth the price of war.[22] Until Vietnam, the United States benefited tremendously from its wars with other nations. World War I and World War II produced economic prosperity for the people of the United States, as well as a sense of national purpose. The Vietnam War did the reverse—it caused an economic crisis and damaged the sense of national purpose. "A Louis Harris poll taken immediately after President Nixon's invasion of Cambodia in May, 1970, revealed that 78 percent of top executives in the five hundred largest firms thought that the President's policies had contributed to the biggest drop in the stock market since the 1929 crash."[22]

It seems to be the case that U.S. multinationals wish to conduct their business abroad without interference from the U.S. government. Of course, they like to use the services of the government agencies, but they do not want to be controlled or regulated by them. Furthermore, the multinationals are more interested in doing business abroad in a peaceful political environment than they are in performing patriotic duties for their country. Perhaps Joseph Schumpeter's contention concerning the peacefulness of modern capitalism is being vindicated. The logic of the transnational system of privilege could very well be replacing the illogic of the battlefield, at least as long as there is no contradiction between profit maximization and peace.

The Ideological Dimension

Whether one subscribes to the Biblical or the evolutionary theory of human creation, the fact remains that human beings have always possessed the twin attributes of needs and imagination. A child born today has the same biological needs and raw power of imagination as a child born thousands of years ago. The specific ways in which human needs are satisfied or the precise questions posed by the imagination are shaped by the levels of material development and socio-cultural advancement. But need as such is not determined by imagination and imagination as such is not determined by needs. Rather, they are two interdependent dimensions of human existence, and it is their interdependence throughout history which has produced the realms of material reality and ideology. For needs seek satisfaction; imagination searches for meaning.

Every socio-economic system has its own ideology, which provides both justification and motivation for human action. Imperialism is no exception. The formulators of U.S. foreign policies toward the underdeveloped world are not the first strategists of imperialism who have had to provide justifications for international domination. The 16th century colonialists were not inhibited by any doctrine of the rights of man. If they treated any of their subjects humanely, it was because they were virtuous themselves and not because the subjects had the right to demand it. After the American and the French revolutions however, the colonialists found themselves in the position of having to justify the use of their power. Thus the 19th century colonialists contended that they were in the business of administering and advancing the masses. They often promised to end their rule as soon as the natives were ready to take care of themselves. Millions of Africans and Asians had to be killed and annual crops had to be burned year after year before the French gave up their civilizing mission and the British abandoned the white man's burden.

In our time imperialists once again fortify themselves with moral sanctions. They justify their actions by claiming to serve the people. However, since imperialism harms the people and defies moral justification, the imperialists then defend themselves by denying the very reality of their actions. When on occasion it becomes ludicrous to deny their domination of other societies, they claim that their actions are educative, liberating and temporary. The brutal consequences of imperialism for the impoverished masses in the subordinated societies do not seem to catch the delicate eyes of the conventional analysts of multinational corporations or U.S. foreign policies. These "men of science" are acting in the long tradition of imperial scholarship. The distinguished scholars of British and French colonialism were also more interested in questions of order and stability in the colonies than the impact of colonialism on the natives.

If the study of politics is about who gets what, when, how and why—that is to say, if politics is concerned with the distribution of resources and its legitimizing ideology—then the study of international politics in this age of complex interdependence must deal with the questions involved in who gets what, when, how and why in interstate relations. The material costs of imperialism come from the public treasury while its benefits go into private hands. And the human cost of imperialism is always paid by those who do not receive its material benefits.

Imperialism is harmful not only to the dominated peoples but also to the vast majority of the citizens in the imperialist society. Barnet and Muller demonstrate in *Global Reach* that by the use of exploitative/manipulative devices such as "transfer pricing" multinational corporations retard the economic development of the poor nations and at the same time cause retrogressive tendencies in their home countries as a result of the transfer of productive and distributive operations from the United States to low wage host countries.

Why then are the imperialist policies justified by society? Why do people submit to the policymakers' call for both material and human sacrifice? What is the source of common motivations between the rulers and the ruled in their pursuit of imperialist policies? How is the attempt to impose values on foreigners justified to the citizens at home? Why do the citizens accept such justifications? How are people rewarded for their sacrifices? Are people ever deceived? How could deception work on a literate and relatively informed population? These questions cannot be comprehended or answered without an understanding of the role of ideology in the formulation and implementation of the imperialist policies.

In the following chapters, we will see how the economic, political, military and ideological dimensions of U.S. imperialism have developed over the last hundred years.

Chapter 2 Footnotes

1. James Caposaso, "Methodological Issues in the Measurement of Inequality, Dependence, and Exploitation," in *Testing Theories of Economic Imperialism*, Steven J. Rose and James R. Kurth (Lexington, Mass.: D.C. Heath & Co., 1974), pp. 87-91.
2. Johan Galtung, *The True Worlds: A Transnational Perspective* (New York: The Free Press, 1980), p. 57.
3. Ibid., p. 400.
4. Ibid., p. 111.
5. Hans J. Morganthou, *Politics Among Nations* (New York: Knopf, 1967).
6. Rupert Emerson, *From Empire to Nation* (Boston: Beacon Press, 1960), pp. 37-89.
7. *Wall Street Journal*, 7 December 1970, p. 1.
8. Karl Marx and Frederick Engels, *The German Ideology* (New York: International Publishers, 1970). p. 64.
9. Richard Barnet and Ronald Muller, *Global Reach* (New York: Simon and Schuster, 1974).
10. Richard Sklar, "Postimperialism: A Class Analysis of Multinational Corporate Expansion," *Comparative Politics* (October 1978), pp. 77-78.
11. Amaury de Riencourt, *The American Empire* (New York: Dell Publsihing Co., 1968). p. 99.
12. Richard Hofstadter, *Social Darwinism in American Thought* (New York: George Braziller, Inc., 1959). p. 184.
13. Seymour Melman, *Pentagon Capitalism* (New York: McGraw-Hill Book Co., 1970), p. 34.
14. de Riencourt, *The American Empire*, p. 107.

15. Ibid.
16. Franz Schurmann, *The Logic of World Power: An Inquiry Into the Origins, Currents, and Contradictions of World Politics* (New York: Pantheon Books, 1974), pp. 536-556.
17. Noam Chomsky and Howard Zinn, eds., *The Pentagon Papers: Critical Essays* (Boston: Beacon Press, 1972).
18. Walt W. Rostow, *The Stages of Economic Growth* (Cambridge: Cambridge University Press, 1969).
19. Michael T. Klare, *Supplying Repression* (New York: The Field Foundation, 1977), pp. 31-40.
20. Ibid., p. 9.
21. Schurmann, *The Logic of World Power* p. 113.
22. Richard Barnet, *The Roots of War* (Baltimore: Penguin Books, 1972), p. 226.
23. Ibid.

CHAPTER 3

THE SPANISH-AMERICAN WAR AND ITS IDEOLOGICAL ROOTS

The Spanish-American War of 1898 should be perceived as the turning point in the development of the United States as an imperialist power in the contemporary world. Historian Frederick Merk maintains that from the time of the Mexican War there were two schools of thought in the United States. One school advocated acquisition of territory in order to increase the nation's wealth and power. The other school stressed the U.S. mission to be the example of democracy and individual liberty. Both traditions had strong roots in U.S. society, but the socioeconomic circumstances of the 1890s favored the expansionist tradition.[1]

In his book *Expansionists of 1898*, Julius Pratt emphasizes social darwinism as the motivating force behind the expansionist tendencies of the period. He maintains that the expansionists of the 1890s took from Herbert Spencer the idea of the endless struggle for survival and defended expansion as a necessity dictated by scientific law. They believed that the refusal of the United States to expand beyond its territorial boundaries would lead to defeat, decay and decline.[2]

Many newspapers and periodicals, including religious journals, employed social darwinist language to describe the U.S. alternatives as expansion or decline.[3] The *Catholic World* "...spoke of the dynamism of the Anglo-Saxon race leading inevitably to territorial expansion."[4] The *Baptist Union* remarked, "The century that is just closing has brought with it great changes. There are no longer any far-off lands...steam and electricity have well-nigh blotted out distance."[5] And the business press emphasized the need for new commercial opportunities in the markets of the world.

Most leaders of public opinion initially opposed imperialism, but they finally came to support the expansionist policies.

> In coming to an opinion about colonial expansion many Americans unquestionably thought of the depressed economic conditions of recent years, the shrinkage of foreign markets resulting from European tariffs, and the prospect of expanded trade if the United States had island colonies as entrepots in the Far East.[6]

Businessmen wanted the government to intervene in Cuba, but it was left to the ministers and the press to mobilize the necessary public support. Preachers described Spanish cruelties to their Sunday listeners; the newspaperman Joseph Pulitzer and William Randolph Hearst made sensational appeals for war against Spain. When the American battleship *Maine* was sunk in Havana harbor, demands for war grew loud and irresistable.

Theodore Roosevelt integrated the economic expansion with ideological considerations and created a logic and a set of responsibilities which made peace itself the consequence of empire. As he put it himself, it was the "American's duty toward the people living in barbarism to see that they are freed from their chains, and we can free them only by destroying barbarism itself." Thus, he concludes "...peace cannot be had until the civilized nations have expanded in some shape over the barbarous nations."[7] In this way the inherent requirements of economic expansion coincided with such religious, racist and reformist drives to remake the world.

In 1894, President McKinley named Theodore Roosevelt Assistant Secretary of the Navy. In that position, Roosevelt was able to put into practice the theories of Admiral Alfred Mahan concerning the inseparability of naval power and maritime commerce. When the United States declared war on Spain, Roosevelt resigned his position to help organize the first U.S. Volunteer Cavalry and soon became its commander.

Thus, in 1898 the U.S. waged a three month war with Spain. It took the Philippine Islands from Spain by treaty. At the same time the Hawaiian Islands were formally annexed. In 1899 it partitioned the Samoan Islands by agreement with Germany and expressed its policy toward western interests in China in the "Open Door" note. In 1900 U.S. soldiers took part in suppressing the Chinese Boxer Rebellion. By 1902 the army had finally suppressed insurrection in the Philippines, and the islands were made a territory of the United States.

The acquisition of Caribbean and Pacific colonies in 1898 as a result of the Spanish-American War marked the real beginning of the United States empire. Fifty years later the U.S. possessed an immense network of military bases around the world. There is convincing evidence that the people of the United States did not want an empire. Nevertheless, it is true that the creation of the U.S. empire was the logical outcome of actions taken by the U.S. government, and it is true that the justifications for these actions were rooted in the structure of beliefs and values of the people of the United States.

A radical change in public perception since the turn of the century is the acceptance of the global involvements of the U.S. as normal. In the great debate concerning annexation of the Philippines, only a few men of power questioned the inherent legitimacy of such an undertaking. As historian William Pomeroy has written,

> One of the most significant aspects of policy was largely unstated in the debate, and was significant pre-

> cisely because it remained unstated and outside the area of conflict. This was the main tendency of American imperialist interests to expand and to concentrate in areas adjacent to the United States, in Canada and in Latin America. The "big stick" policy of armed intervention in the Caribbean, Central America and Mexico did not arouse protest on a scale that the conquest of the Philippines did. More important, there was no objection to indirect domination of the countries in these areas, although the effects of this on their peoples were virtually the same as the effect on the colonialized Filipino people.[8]

Though there was strong opposition to acquisition of the Philippines, many critics were not against imperialism for moral reasons, their point being, rather, that this particular adventure was unnecessary and unprofitable. The opposition, thus, was based more on questions of feasibility than objective.

In late 19th century England, the term imperialism developed two distinct and contradictory meanings. One meaning regarded imperialism as compatible with the freedom of small nations. Another meaning viewed it as constant extension of territory and subjection of other peoples. As the liberal lawyer R.T. Reid contended,

> ...if imperialism means sober pride in the great Empire we control, a most earnest desire to knit together in the bonds of friendship the various populations that belong to it, a firm determination to preserve the integrity of our Empire at all costs, and the using of the means of advancing civilization among all kinds and conditions of men—then there is no one more of an imperialist than I am. But if it means departing from the old and honoured tradition of this country to respect the freedom of other nations, even if they be small nations and to advance rather than to retard liberty...then it is the duty of every honest citizen of this country to destroy that spirit, because otherwise that spirit is certain to destroy us.[9]

In the United States imperialism did not contain two contradictory sets of ideas. Both the supporters and the opponents of imperialism used the term to mean overseas expansion of U.S. political control and aspiration for the status of a world power. In the years 1898-1900, when the debate over the annexation of the Philippine Islands was going on, national emotion had reached such a climax that overseas expansion was regarded by many citizens of the United States as the "Manifest Destiny" of the U.S., the preordained course of the natural law of growth. Some considered imperial expansion a civilizing duty just as some in England did; others viewed it as an economic necessity.

The economic argument contended that excessive savings and the accumulation of goods were apt to cause crises. There were three possible ways of dealing with these crises. The first was the socialist solution of increased consumption and elimination of private savers and investors. This solution existed only in theory; it had no significant political force behind it. The second solution was to create new economic demands at home. The third solution was to employ capital in other countries and procure new markets for surplus goods. The imperialists maintained that the creation of new economic demands at home was at best an insufficient solution to the growing problem of excessive savings and accumulation of goods. Thus, overseas expansion was widely regarded as the only effective solution to the problem of overproduction. For many who accepted this argument, internal social stability and domestic prosperity figured much more prominently in sanctifying imperialism than did military glory and triumphs abroad.

The opposition to imperialism was, by and large, based on constitutional and ideological considerations. Carl Schurz, a prominent leader of the American Anti-Imperialist League, summarized the fundamental contention of the anti-imperialist arguments in the style of the Declaration of Inpendence.

> We hold that the policy known as imperialism is hostile to liberty and tends towards militarism and evil from which it has been our glory to be free. We regret that it has become necessary in the land of Washington and Lincoln to reaffirm that all men of whatever

> race or color are entitled to life, liberty, and the pursuit of happiness.[10]

The proponents of imperialism held that the Constitution cannot (and should not) be binding beyond the territorial boundaries of the United States. But they did not openly defend imperialism as a matter of policy because the word had negative connotations to the public. In the presidential election of 1900 President McKinley, in spite of his obvious imperialist policies, never made support for imperialism a part of his platform.[11]

It is easy to look back and regard the Great Debate of the 1890s as an argument between fellow imperialists who differed over tactics and instrumentality. But those who took part in the debate over territorial expansion were convinced that the issues had great significance for the future of the United States. It was believed by both sides of the argument that a policy of overseas territorial acquisition would be the beginning of a new era in the life of the nation. Those who supported the policy of expansion maintained that the industrial economy of the United States demanded foreign markets for U.S. goods and capital, and that the security of these markets required political and territorial control. Those who opposed the expansionist policy held that overseas political and territorial control would involve the U.S. in European power politics and violate the moral and constitutional tradition of the United States.[12] They believed that the demands of the U.S. economy would best be served through peaceful trade and commerce.

The Great Debate must be understood in the context of its time. The participants in the debate were not concerned with economic imperialism but rather with the expansion of United States sovereignty to such overseas territories as the Samoan Islands, Hawaii, Puerto Rico, Cuba and the Philippines. To comprehend fully the societal milieu of the Great Debate, it is necessary to understand the sociological conditions and ideological notions which influenced the U.S. political scene for a quarter century prior to the Spanish-American War.

The frontier on the North American continent vanished with the battle of Wounded Knee Creek in 1890, if not before, but the frontier consciousness continued to be an integral part of the U.S. ethos. The people of the United States have always tended to view expansion as an indispensable part of their socio-economic life. In a language well known to contemporary observers of U.S. foreign policy, John Quincy Adams wrote the following words in the 1830s, "In looking forward to the probable course of events, it is scarcely possible to resist the conviction that the annexation of Cuba to our Federal Republic will be indispensable to the continuance and integrity of the Union itself."[13]

In the decades following the Civil War, the United States was a vast theater of the struggle for existence and survival of the fittest. It was an age of rapid socio-economic change. The nation was being transformed from an agricultural to a manufacturing society, and the capitalists became interested in markets rather than land. Although the nation was rich in natural resources, there were some important raw materials which did not exist in the United States or were in short supply. Among them were rubber, silk, jute, tin, nickel, nitrate, cork, manganese and tungsten. There were also such foodstuffs as coffee, cocoa, bananas, sugar, olive oil and coconuts for which there was a growing market at home. The United States was not yet involved in European power politics, but the capitalists were aware that to have a share in the control of these resources the country had to become active in world markets.

The Merchant Marine of the United States suffered a drastic setback in the decades following the Civil War. The share of imports and exports carried under the U.S. flag fell from 66.5 percent in 1865 to 7.1 percent in 1900.[14] One of the men who responded to this rapid decline in maritime commerce was Admiral Alfred Mahan. He advocated the inseparability of naval power and maritime commerce and maintained that they were both necessary for the strength and prosperity of the United States. He denounced the myth of isolationism and predicted that Americans were going to get involved in world politics whether they wanted to or not. Since such assertions had no large following among the general public, Mahan had to reiterate that there was "no aggressive action in our pious souls."[15]

These developments in the realm of economic interests were paralleled by the popularization of certain notions in the realm of ideology. In the midst of rapid economic growth and unprecedented acumulation of wealth, systematic oppression of the underclasses, labor unrest and high unemployment were the ingredients of the socio-political scene. In the midst of industrialization and the vast expansion of productive capacity, the citizens were becoming more insecure and wanting. Capitalism had begun to end the ageless conditions of objective scarcity at the expense of intensifying subjective scarcity. It was fundamentally in response to these contradictions that during the last third of the 19th century a number of social thinkers in the U.S. undertook the ideological task of transfering the Darwinian evolutionary theory of survival to the social universe in order to justify and exalt inequality, imperialism, war, conquest and the racial superiority of the Teutonic peoples.

One of the first protagonists of this point of view was John W. Draper (1811-1882), a professor of chemistry and physiology. He maintained that "social advancement is as completely under the control of natural law as is the bodily growth of an individual."[16] Thus, it is possible to predict with scientific accuracy "the inevitable course through which a nation must pass."[17] It is therefore in the province of statesmen "to determine how change should be provided for in the political institutions, and what is the true nature of the law by which they shall be modified."[18] Since life is "influenced by physical agents and is...under the control of law," Draper continues, "there are physical boundaries beyond which society cannot pass and ends that no human legislation can accomplish."[19]

Draper puts much emphasis on the formative influence on the United States of climate, immigration, and "the rational course of national development."[20] Ideas govern the world, while "nature has prepared the path along which the course must be run."[21] Thus, nature had made it possible for the U.S. to develop without "vast ecclesiastical establishments," which resulted in intellectual freedom and a belief in the universal superiority of their achievement. The fundamental idea in the United States is that,

> there shall exist on this continent one Republic, great and indivisible, whose grandeur shall eclipse the grandeur of Rome...so ruling in truth, in wisdom, in justice, in force, that every human being, no matter how obscure or desolate he may find in it a refuge and protector; that every government, from the Atlantic Ocean...to the Chinese Seas, no matter how strong it may be shall listen with attention to its suggestions.[22]

Then he goes on to explain that the creation and development of the United States was determined by a universal law and moral imperative,

> There is a course through which we must go. Let us cast from ourselves the untrue, the unworthy belief that the will of man determines the events of this world. National life...is shaped by a stern logic of events.[23]

Draper concludes his analysis of the U.S. destiny with the contention that there are but three powers that can organize the world: theology, literature and science. Europe exhausted the first, and the Chinese failed with the second, but the United States is capable of succeeding through the applications of science because science can be communicated universally if its socio-political organization, while being committed to equal opportunity for all, is based on superiority and subordination.[24] Thus, according to Draper, the United States had a destiny to pursue a policy of horizontal expansion in order to organize the world through the application of science and to rule it with truth, justice and force. Nature was with the United States; what was needed to guarantee the success of this noble mission was good statesmanship.

Lewis H. Morgan, the pioneer U.S. anthropologist, was another thinker who unveiled a universal scientific mission for his country. Morgan has been more influential than Draper in defining the conceptual framework which came to be used to formulate scientific explanations of both domestic and foreign objectives. He develops an idealistic and materialistic theory of evolution in order to show that "the principal institutions of mankind have been developed from a few primary germs of thought; and that the course and manner of their development were predetermined, as well as restricted within narrow limits of divergence, by the natural logic of the human mind and the necessary limitations of its power."[25] Then Morgan tries to demonstrate that only inventions and discoveries cause the advance of civilization from one stage of natural development to another. "With the production of inventions and discoveries, and with the growth of institutions, the human mind necessarily grew and expanded."[26] Thus, according to Morgan, civilization is ultimately measured in terms of technological advancement, which is the foundation of economic institutions in any given stage of natural development. The economic institutions, in turn, determine the superstructure of politics. He maintains that at the present stage of civilization the passion for property, which has reached a new level of intensity with technological advancement, dominates the minds of men and determines the nature of their economic and political institutions. Analyzing the principle of private property, he declares that

> there is something grandly impressive in a principle which has wrought out civilization by assiduous application from small beginnings; from the narrow head, which expresses the thought in the brain of a savage, to the smelting of iron ore, which represents the higher intelligence of the barbarian, and, finally, to the railway train in motion, which may be called the triumph of civilization.[27]

This view of human civilization led Morgan to contend that U.S. society, based on private property and representative democracy, constituted the highest stage of civilization yet achieved. This achievement, however, was not the ultimate stage. Greater egalitarianism within the U.S. socio-economic system and its horizontal expansion was destined to lead to the next natural stage of civilization. He was certain that "democracy in government, brotherhood in society, equality in rights and privileges, and universal education, foreshadow the next higher plane of society."[28] Thus, Morgan restated the belief that the United States, with its technology and democracy, possessed the key to the salvation of mankind. This was the destiny of the U.S. and the eventual result could not be in doubt. Only the timing of this natural development was subject to human intervention and fortuitous circumstances.

For both Draper and Morgan the eventual global expansion of the U.S. socio-economic system was guaranteed by nature. The province of statesmanship was limited to the reconciliation of social action with the natural order. These ideological aspirations were presented as scientific facts. Society was an organism; nationalism was an expansive force; and science, as the key to the understanding of civilization, provided the means of uncovering the laws of human behavior and the realizing of world hegemony for the United States. And all this was the natural result of representative democracy and the institution of private property. These deterministic and ethnocentric notions had a profound impact not only on the conscience of many U.S. citizens, but also on the development of both the content and methodology of social sciences in the United States.

The last quarter of the 19th century was an age of rapid economic change in the United States. It was during this period that Darwin's and Spencer's ideas were popularized. It was an age in which the prevailing political mood was conservative. As Richard Hofstadter observes,

> Challenges to this dominant conservatism were never absent, but the characteristic feeling was that the country had seen enough agitation over political issues in the period before the Civil War, that the time had now come for acquiescence and acquisition, for the development and enjoyment of the great continent that was being settled and the immense new industries that were springing up.[29]

Spencer's system of thought was conceived in the age of steel, steam engines, competition, exploitation and commitment to unlimited material expansion. His social ideas are intelligible only in the context of his general philosophy. The appeal of his social theories in the United States was largely due to his synthetic integration of knowledge. "The aim of Spencer's synthesis was to gain in one coherent structure the latest findings of physics and biology."[30] The principle of the conservation of energy was developed in the same period that the idea of natural selection was formulated by Darwin.

The conservation of energy, which Spencer called "the persistence of force," constituted the basis of his philosophical system. Everywhere man observes the incessant redistribution of matter and motion, apportioned between evolution and dissolution.

> From the persistence of force, Spencer inferred that anything which is homogeneous is inherently unstable, since the different effects of persistent force upon its various parts must cause differences to arise in their future development. Thus the homogeneous will inevitably develop into the heterogeneous. Here is the key to universal evolution. This progress from homogeneity to heterogeneity.... Here the pattern of universal rhythm comes into play: dissolution follows evolution, disintegration follows integration. In an organism this phase is represented by death and decay, but in society by the establishment of a stable, harmonious, completely adapted state, in which 'evolution can end only in the establishment of the greatest perfection and the most complete happiness.'[31]

This positivistic view of society, as Hofstadter notes, "might have been totally unacceptable in the United States, had it not also been bound up with an important concession to religion in the form of Spencer's doctrine of the Unknowable."[32] Thus, Spencer gave a definite affirmative answer to the all-important question of the time concerning the reconcilability of religion and science. He went even further and gave "assurance for all future ages that, whatever science might learn about the world, the true sphere of religion—worship of the Unknowable—is by its very nature inviolable."[33] Spencer never questioned the primacy of ethical considerations in the life of the society. He said "my ultimate purpose, lying behind all proximate purposes, has been that of finding for the principles of right and wrong in conduct at large, a scientific basis."[34]

Spencer might have had a noble purpose in mind, but his social philosophy came to be an effective rationalization for inequality at home and expansion abroad. He categorically rejected any compulsory or state-supported action to aid the underprivileged. He was only in favor of private charity to the unfit, and even that more for elevating the character and demonstrating the altruism of the donor than for improving the plight of the poor. "There cannot be more good done than that of letting social progress go on unhindered; yet an immensity of mischief may be done in the way of disturbing, and distorting and repressing, by policies carried out in pursuit of erroneous conceptions."[35] Thus, an adequate theory must refrain from violating the selection principle by "the artificial preservation of those least able to take care of themselves."[36]

The principle of selection was close to the heart of the United States, particularly to those who were benefiting most from rapid expansion and the new exploitative methods. John D. Rockefeller declared,

> The growth of a large business is merely a survival of the fittest.... The American Beauty rose can be produced in the splendor and fragrance which brings cheer to its beholder only by sacrificing the early buds which grow up around it. This is not an evil tendency in business. It is merely the working-out of a law of nature and a law of God.[37]

And Andrew Carnegie, a disciple and close friend of Spencer, revealed his view of Spencer as follows,

> I remember that light came as in a flood and all was clear. Not only had I got rid of theology and the supernatural, but I had found the truth of evolution. "All is well since all grows better," became my motto, my true source of comfort. Man was not created with an instinct for his own degradation, but from the lower he had risen to the higher forms. Nor is there any conceivable end to his march to perfection. His face is turned to the light; he stands in the sun and looks upward.[38]

Even the Supreme Court's interpretation of the Constitution converged with Spencer's philosophy in turning back the tide of social reform. It was this convergence which finally "inspired Mr. Justice Holmes (himself an admirer of Spencer) to protest that 'the Fourteenth Amendment does not enact Mr. Herbert Spencer's Social Statics'."[39]

Spencer reached the peak of his U.S. popularity in 1882 when he visited the United States. Many notable men of letters, science, politics, theology and business paid tribute to him. He assured his U.S. friends of their future when he told them that they might "reasonably look forward to a time when they will have produced a civilization grander than any the world has known."[40] On the occasion of his departure from the United States, Spencer held the hands of Andrew Carnegie and Edward Livinston Youman, a popular spokesman for the scientific world outlook, and said, "Here are my two best American friends."[41] This gesture of personal friendship symbolized the unity of science and the business civilization of the United States.

Footnotes: Chapter 3

1. Frederick Merk, *Manifest Destiny and Mission in American History: A Reinterpretation* (New York: Knopf, 1963), pp. 228-236.
2. Julius W. Pratt, *Expansionists of 1898: The Acquisition of Hawaii and the Spanish Islands* (Magnolia, Mass.: Peter Smith, Inc., 1936), pp. 230-316.
3. Ernest May, *American Imperialism: A Speculative Essay* (New York: Atheneum, 1968), p. 193.
4. Ibid.
5. Ibid.
6. Ibid., p. 194.
7. William A. Williams, *The Tragedy of American Diplomacy* (New York: Delta, 1962), p. 72.
8. William J. Pomeroy, *American Neo-Colonialism: Its Emergence in the Philippines and Asia* (New York: International Publishers, 1970), pp. 9-10.
9. R. Koebner and H.D. Schmidt, *Imperialism* (Cambridge: Cambridge University Press), p. 230.
10. Ibid., p. 240.
11. David Healy, *U.S. Expansionism: The Imperialist Urge in the 1890s* (Madison: The University of Wisconsin Press, 1970), pp. 144-147.
12. Ibid., pp. 248-255.
13. Harold U. Faulkner, *American Economic History* (New York: Harper & Row, 1960), pp.539-540.
14. Ibid., p. 25.
15. Charles and Mary Beard, *A Basic History of the United States* (New York: Doubleday, Doran & Co., 1945), p. 339.
16. John W. Draper, *Thoughts on the Future Civil Policy of America* (New York: Garland Publishers, 1867), p. iii.
17. Ibid., p. iv.
18. Ibid., p. 59.
19. Ibid., p. 36.
20. Ibid., p. 37.
21. Ibid., p. 46.
22. Ibid., p. 82.
23. Ibid.
24. Ibid., p. 197.
25. Lewis H. Morgan, *Ancient Society: Researches in the Lines of Human Progress From Savagery Through Barbarism to Civilization* (Chicago: C.H. Kerr, 1877), p. 17.

26. Ibid., p. 18.
27. Ibid., p. vii.
28. Ibid., p. 553.
29. Hofstadter, *Social Darwinism,* p. 5.
30. Ibid., p. 36.
31. Ibid., p. 37.
32. Ibid.
33. Ibid., p. 38.
34. Ibid., p. 40.
35. Ibid.
36. Ibid.
37. Ibid., p. 45.
38. Ibid.
39. Ibid., p. 47.
40. Ibid., p. 59.
41. Ibid., p. 61.

CHAPTER 4

WORLD WAR I AND WOODROW WILSON: THE ANTI-COLONIAL IMPERIALIST

The problems which impose limitations on economic expansion are often socio-political. In the 19th century, as Hannah Arandt has written,

> Imperialism was born when the ruling class in capitalist production came up against national limitations to its economic expansion. The bourgeoisie turned to politics out of economic necessity; for if it did not want to give up the capitalist system whose inherent law is constant economic growth, it had to impose this law upon its home governments and to proclaim expansion to be an ultimate political goal of foreign policy.[1]

As we saw in Chapter 2, imperialism in the 19th century was touched off by the existence of surplus capital which could not find productive investment within the national borders. The export of capital to a foreign country is soon followed by the export of government power. The export of capital is the business of a small group of people while the export of government power must be conducted in the name of national interest. Imperialism was caused by the incongruity of the nation-state with the economic and industrial developments of the period. Thus, while imperialism was driven by economic necessity, it was also driven by the politics of expansion for expansion's sake.

Imperialism is not the same as expansionism. A nation does not become an empire simply through expanding interests or even by direct or indirect conquest. When a nation becomes an empire a new realm of political ideology comes into being. "A nation is primarily concerned with national interests. Empires, in addition to pursuing their own interests as nations, also pursue goals deriving from the imperial ideology, which are frequently incomprehensible in terms of national interest."[2]

An obvious consequence of foreign investment is the identification of the interests of a small group of financiers and industrialists with the national interest. The greater the amount of investment beyond the national boundaries, the more urgent the need for the expansion of government power. For, as a general rule, "a never ending accumulation of property must be based on a never ending accumulation of power.... The limitless process of capital accumulation needs the political structure of so unlimited a power that it can protect growing property by constantly growing more powerful."[3]

Until the outbreak of World War I the domination of most of the world by Western European powers was, for all practical purposes, unquestioned. The United States and Japan had begun their imperialistic activities, but "politically, economically, and culturally, it was a world which centered to a striking degree on the peoples of Europe and their offshoots."[4]

In the late 19th century European expansion seemed the natural order of things. Moral condemnation of imperialism was limited to a few socialist and liberal elements. Those in control of the political and economic institutions of the Western societies believed in white supremacy. There was some criticism of the methods of expansion and domination, but there was very little attack on the colonial system itself. The distortion ot Darwinian concepts to give scientific validity to racism and exploitation provided justification for what was already being practiced on a global level.

In the political/legal realm, at the end of World War I the Allied peacemakers created the Mandates System to deal with the German colonies and the Arab areas which the European powers had been dividing up amongst themselves during the war.

> The Mandates System, invented to deal with these territories, is fair game for both idealist and cynic since it represented a new and enlightened approach to colonialism and was also a practical expedient for sharing the spoils of war among the victors without too grave a violation of non-annexation pledges. Taking the existing colonial system as a model, it imposed certain standards and restrictions on it and subjected the Mandatory Powers to a modest but unprecedented international supervision—which they, no doubt, assumed would be exercised primarily within the family.[5]

Beside the Mandates System, the Allied powers explicitly agreed in Article 23 of the League Covenant "to secure just treatment of the native inhabitants of territories under their control." The only case in which the League took this commitment seriously was the issue of slavery and forced labor. The question of self-determination, which was so close to Woodrow Wilson's heart, did not involve any concern with imperialism. The commitment to national self-determination was clearly understood to be limited to Europe, even though Wilson gave it the sound of universality in his ringing phrase "to make the world safe for democracy."

> In the Paris peace negotiations colonial issues, save for the Mandates System, played an insignificant role for him. Of the famous Fourteen Points only the fifth made any mention of the colonies, calling for a free and impartial adjustment of colonial claims, based

> upon the principle that 'the interests of the populations concerned must have equal weight with the equitable claims of the government whose title is to be determined.' It is symbolic of the times that the man who set out to make the world safe for democracy went no further than to suggest that the interests—not the national desires—of the colonial peoples should be lifted to an equality with the claims of their alien rulers.[6]

To be sure, the acceptance of self-determination as a guiding principle in the peace conference had a profound impact on the developing nationalism in the colonies. This impact was an unintended consequence of the rhetoric and overconfidence of the Allies, particularly Woodrow Wilson. They announced that self-determination was a valid principle, and the success of the Russian Revolution completely cemented the principle in the consciousness of the colonized.

> While the Western Allies were understandably reluctant to see the principle carried seriously beyond Europe, the Bolsheviks not only made use of it at home but found it an ideal instrument for the confusion of their enemies and the incitement to revolutionary action of the imperialistically downtrodden. The formal transformation of the Russian Empire into an egalitarian multinational federation echoed far beyond the borders and gave new life and direction to the anti-imperialist forces.[7]

The ideology of U.S. imperialism was shaped by the Wilson Administration in response to both the requirements of capitalist expansion and the upheavals of world politics during the 1910s. World War I and the Bolshevik Revolution were the twin events with a decisive impact on U.S. foreign policies, but these events by themselves do not tell the whole story. To comprehend this ideology, the need for expansion and the pursuit of glory must also be considered as realities of world politics. In the late 1910s Wilson formulated a strategy for constructing a world order based on liberal capitalist internationalism. This conception was not new in U.S. foreign policy, but it was Woodrow Wilson who transformed the concept into an ideology. This ideology had,

> at one and the same time, the varied but related tasks of countering Germany's atavistic imperialism, of answering the moral and economic expansion of the liberal American nation-state. The crucial importance of Wilsonianism, then, in the context of 20th century American foreign relations, lies in the fact that the Wilson Administration first defined the American national interest in liberal-internationalist terms in response to war and social revolution, the two dominant political factors of our time.[8]

Wilson believed that the United States ought to disseminate its moral, political and economic doctrines in order to create a new world order. He did not conceive of the U.S. being imperialist toward other nations. In his liberal ideology, imperialism and militarism had no place. "The President never doubted that American liberal values were the wave of the future in world politics. Soon the whole world would follow the lead of the United States to the establishment of an international system of peaceful commercial and political order."[9] Thus, for Wilson, U.S. liberalism was universally applicable and its acceptance by other nations was a prerequisite for world peace. Given the fact that U.S. society, unlike the rest of the world, had no experience with preliberal values and classes, "Wilson's ideology permitted him to conceive of himself as acting, at one and the same time, with perfect internal consistency, as the defender of American national interests and as the champion of liberal-internationalism."[10]

Wilson's ideology permitted him to participate in the illiberal system of world politics and, at the same time, claim to be the carrier of values able to liberalize that very system. Wilson's strategy for achieving his objective had two dimensions. On the one hand, Wilson sought to absorb the conflicting elements of world politics under the League of Nations. On the other hand, he was ready to use force to impose his values whenever he saw the need. The liberal League was supposed to help Americanize the world by means of reform, without revolution; Wilson's readiness to use force was a response to those who rejected his ideological solution in principle.

The Wilsonian politics of gradual liberalism was opposed to both traditional liberalism and revolutionary radicalism. When Wilson entered World War I against Germany he made the war seem the precondition of peace and progress in the future. And "after failing to prevent the triumph of Russian Bolshevism, the Wilson Administration continued its limited efforts, by means of intervention and diplomacy, to end the single-party rule of the Bolsheviks and hopefully to bring Russia back to the lost liberalism of the March Revolution."[11]

The uniqueness of Wilsonian ideology was that it was meant to be *in* but not *of* the existing system of international politics. It was a vehicle for ending traditional imperialism and preventing the growth of revolutionary radicalism by reforming world politics from within. Therefore, the United States could "participate in a world war alongside a major European military alliance and, at the same time, hope to remake the alliance into an agency of liberal-international reform."[12] This notion of the U.S. mission made it possible for Wilson "to reconcile the rapid growth of the economic and military power of the United States with what he conceived to be America's unselfish service to humanity."[13]

This reconciliation, however, never left the realm of theory. In practice the Wilsonian ideology was the ideology of economic and political expansion. Wilson was aware of the need for such expansion when he began his campaign for the presidency. In 1912 he told the Virginia General Assembly that "we are making more manufactured goods than we can consume ourselves...and now, if we are not going to stifle economically, we have got to find our way out into the great international exchanges of the world."[14] For Wilson, expansion in the interest of U.S. capitalism was in complete harmony with his vision of a liberal world order. He seemed certain that in a competitive world of free trade and technological efficiency "the skill of American workmen would dominate the markets of all the globe."[15] When Wilson ran for re-election in 1916 he took pride in what he had done for American commercial interests abroad. He "stressed the aid given by the Federal Reserve Act, the Federal Trade Commission, and the Commerce Department to American exporters, and called on nation's business leaders to rise to their global opportunities."[16]

Conservative Republicans criticized Wilson's expansionist policy because it lowered tariffs as a means of increasing exports. With the exception of the radical elements hardly anyone questioned the ideology of expansion in principle. Socialists and some liberals maintained that "there was no real surplus to export, but only those goods which the lower classes were not able to consume at existing price and income levels."[17] The radical elements also objected to the Wilsonian ideology because they saw it as imperialistic and war-oriented. Wilson rejected both conservative and radical critics and maintained that it was possible to pursue expansion without such imperialist practices as protectionism, militarism and war. He saw his expansionist policies as a vehicle for serving a suffering humanity. In this ideology he combined liberalism, capitalism and missionary nationalism,

> America has stood in the years past for that sort of political understanding among men which would let every man feel that his rights were the same as those of another and as good as those of another, and the mission of America in the field of the world's commerce is to be the same; that when an American comes into that competition he comes without any arms that would enable him to conquer by force, but only with those peaceful influences of intelligence, a desire to serve, a knowledge of what he is about, before which everything softens and yields, and renders itself subject. That is the mission of America, and my interest, so far as my small part in American affairs is concerned, is to lend every bit of intelligence I have to this interesting, this vital, this all-important matter of releasing the intelligence of America for the service of mankind.[18]

And this is how he explained his expansionist ideology to a group of businessmen,

> Eyes to the horizons of business; do not look too close at the little processes with which you are concerned, but let your thoughts and your imaginations run abroad throughout the whole world, and with the inspiration of the thought that you are Americans and are meant to carry liberty and justice and the principles of humanity wherever you go, go out and sell goods that will make the world more comfortable and more happy, and convert them to the principles of America.[19]

During the first administration of Woodrow Wilson the export trade had begun to make the United States a leading economic power in the world. It had turned the United States from a debtor to a creditor nation.

The Wilsonian strategy for peace and prosperity in the world had two inter-related objectives: first, to reintegrate Germany into a stable western unity under the moral leadership of the United States; and second, to restructure the process of economic competition among the advanced western nations in the underdeveloped world in order to maintain the Open Door in a rational manner. In 1914 Colonel House explained this strategy to a group of British leaders as follows,

> My plan is that if England, the United States, Germany and France will come to an understanding concerning investments by their citizens in underdeveloped countries, much good and profit will come to their citizens as well as to the countries needing development. Stability would be brought about, investments would become safe, and low rates of interest might be established.[20]

Thus, the people of the underdeveloped areas were placed in the context of the international liberal order sought by the Wilson Administration. Wilson never questioned the structural inequalities between the developed and underdeveloped areas of the world. He opposed the imperialism of territorial annexations, but he accepted the moral superiority and world predominance of the West as just and natural. Wilson was motivated by the needs of U.S. capitalism and his faith in the progressive values of liberal internationalism. He blamed the war on the "atavistic and irrational patterns of European national behavior and retained a faith in the peaceful and orderly potential of international capitalism in particular."[21] Thus, it was the duty of the United States to "undertake to be the champions of humanity and the rights of man. Without that ideal there would be nothing that would distinguish America from her predecessors in the history of nations."[22]

Wilson considered Germany's submarine warfare a threat to the liberal world order he was committed to fostering. He never failed to make it clear that the United States was ready to fight for her rights, which were identical with universal human rights. A few months before entering the war against Germany in 1916, he said, "America ought to keep out of this war. She ought to keep out of this war at the sacrifice of everything except this single thing upon which her character and history are founded, her sense of humanity and justice... Valor is self-respecting...Valor withholds itself from all small implications and entanglements and waits for the great opportunity when the sword will flash as if it carried the light of heaven upon its blade."[23]

Woodrow Wilson decided to "teach the South American Republics to elect good men." He began by intervening in the Mexican Revolution. A historian has described the result in the following words,

> An election was held in October. But its results, being favorable to General Huerta, were, Wilson decided, not a genuine expression of the will of the people.... In his complaint that the elections were 'irregularly conducted' he was right, but it only showed his ignorance of Mexico that he would have troubled to make such a complaint. The electoral machinery was treated by both sides as a tired and flagging joke and was kept in existence only out of puzzled good nature because, for some reason quite incomprehensible, it seemed to give pleasure to the President of the United States.[24]

Wilson thought otherwise. He had "gone to Mexico to serve mankind." He was so convinced of his righteousness that the contrary facts could not dispel the myth he had accepted as reality.

Woodrow Wilson was re-elected in 1916 because he kept the country out of war. But he entered the war three months later. In this short period he went from "official neutrality to complete dictation of the terms of surrender, for peace, and for the postwar organization of the nations." After the war he supported the League of Nations and chose the name Covenant for its charter. He wanted to abolish all partial alliances and establish a single institution to deal with world problems. He wanted all or nothing.

> There can be no compromise. No halfway decision would be tolerable. No halfway decision is conceivable. These are the ends for which the associated people of the world are fighting and which must be conceded them before there can be peace: I. The destruction of every arbitrary power anywhere that can separately, secretly, and of its single choice disturb the peace of the world.... II. The settlement of every question, whether of territory, of sovereignty, of economic arrangement, or of political relationship, upon the basis of the free acceptance of that settlement by the people immediately concerned.... III. The consent of all nations to be governed in their conduct towards each other by the same principles of honor and of respect for the common law of civilized society that govern the individual citizens of all modern nations in their relations with one another.... IV. The establishment of an organization of peace which shall make it certain that the combined power of free nations will check every invasion of right....[25]

In his May 1969 speech on Vietnam Richard Nixon paraphrased the Wilsonian imperial creed,

> What we want for South Vietnam is not the important thing. What is important is what the people of South

> Vietnam want for themselves. We are willing to agree to neutrality if that is what the South Vietnamese people freely choose. We are prepared to accept any government in South Vietnam that results from the free choice of the South Vietnamese people themselves. We ask only that the decision reflect the free choice of the people concerned...(the kind of settlement) which will permit the South Vietnamese people to determine freely their own political future. Our basic terms are very simple: mutual withdrawal of non-South Vietnamese forces from South Vietnam, and free choice for the people of South Vietnam.[26]

The words freedom and choice are in every sentence. The price the South Vietnamese had to pay to be free constitutes an ugly page in U.S. history.

The contradictions between professed values and the actual practices cannot be dismissed as deception. These contradictions are rooted in the nature of U.S. imperialism. What happened in Vietnam was that the massiveness and the failure of the United States' involvement unmasked the contradictions more clearly than any other case had. It made a significant segment of the U.S. population see, for the first time, what kind of freedom their foreign-policy makers had in mind for the wretched of the earth. The contradictions were there when President McKinley sent the troops to civilize the Filipinos, when President Wilson sent troops to Mexico to demand free elections, when President Eisenhower ordered the Central Intelligence Agency to engineer the overthrow of popular nationalist governments in Iran and Guatemala, when President Kennedy approved the Bay of Pigs invasion and when President Johnson sent the Marines to the Dominican Republic to destroy a popular rebellion. An analysis of the post-World War II developments will demonstrate that this self-righteous ideology and the resultant contradictions continued to exist in the vastly expanded arena of U.S. imperialist operations.

Footnotes: Chapter 4

1. Hannah Arendt, *Imperialism* (New York: Harcourt, Brace and World, Inc., 1968), p. vi.

2. Franz Schurmann, *The Logic of World Power: An Inquiry Into the Origins, Currents, and Contradictions of World Politics* (New York: Pantheon Books, 1974), pp. 16-17.

3. Ibid., p. 23.

4. Rupert Emerson, *From Empire to Nation* (Boston: Beacon Press, 1960), p. 22.

5. Ibid., p. 24.

6. Ibid., p. 35.

7. Ibid., p. 26.

8. N. Gordon Levin, Jr., *Woodrow Wilson and World Politics* (New York: Oxford University Press, 1970), pp. 1-2.

9. Ibid., p. 3.

10. Ibid., p. 5.

11. Ibid., p. 7.

12. Ibid., p. 8.

13. Ibid.

14. Ibid., p. 14.

15. Ibid.

16. Ibid., p. 16.

17. Ibid.

18. Ibid., p. 17.

19. Ibid., p. 16.

20. Ibid., p. 24.

21. Ibid., p. 32.

22. Ibid., p. 34.

23. Ibid., p. 35.

24. Garry Wills, *Nixon Agonistes* (New York: Signet, 1970), p. 396.

25. Ibid., p. 419.

26. Ibid., p. 393.

CHAPTER 5

POST WORLD WAR II AND U.S. GLOBAL EXPANSION

The ideology of U.S. imperialism contains a myth which is widely accepted by the people of the United States. According to this myth the autonomy of each individual in a civil society is challenged by the autonomy of the next individual, with consequent friction, right clashing with right, privilege threatening privilege. The role of government is to adjudicate such conflicts without having unlimited power over the individual. Thus the function of government in the realm of politics is equivalent to the function of the free market in the realm of economics. However, when the majority or a large part of the population does not accept a particular action of the state as the manifestation of national will, the state claims that the national will is not always what the people want but sometimes what they ought to want. That is to say, the national will is not always identical with national destiny.

Richard Nixon was as much committed to the dictates of national destiny as Woodrow Wilson. On November 3, 1969, Nixon said, "Let me be quite blunt. Our fighting men are not going to be worn down; our negotiators are not going to be talked down; our allies are not going to be let down. The peace that we will be able to achieve will be due to the fact that Americans, when it really counted, did not buckle, did not run away, but stood fast so that the enemy knew that it had no choice except to negotiate."[1] Wilson himself put it more eloquently, "I wish there were some great orator who could go about and make men drunk with this spirit of self-sacrifice."[2]

This puritan trait has shown up again and again. Wilson said of the U.S. entry into World War I, "The force of America is the force of moral principle...there is nothing else that she loves, and...there is nothing else for which she will contend."[3] This self-righteousness was not unique to Wilson. Dean Rusk said of Vietnam, "We have no quarrel with the Communists, all our quarrels are on behalf of other people."[4] Nixon has uttered his version of the noble intention of the U.S. foreign wars, "The United States has suffered over one million casualties in four wars in this century. Whatever faults we may have as a nation, we have asked nothing for ourselves in return for these sacrifices."[5] And when he was in Vietnam this is what he said to the U.S. troops, "Out here in this dreary, difficult war, I think history will record that this may have been one of America's finest hours."[6]

This puritanical self-righteousness has often been used as a justification for the United States view of underdevelopment in the Third World. Since World War II U.S. economic policies toward the underdeveloped world have been determined by the dictates of U.S. imperialist ideology and/or the interests of corporations and geopolitical strategists. The formulators of these policies comprise the most powerful political and economic elites in the United States. These elites have been responsible for the creation of an ideological consensus which U.S. leaders from Harry Truman to Jimmy Carter have operated under, and upon which they have been dependent for their ascension to power. In addition, both the short-run and long-run objectives of U.S. policies toward the underdeveloped world have reflected this ideological consensus and the corporate interests which it represents.[7]

While the post-war presidents have employed different styles of rhetoric and different methods of domination, the goal of their policies has remained consistent—creation of a world open for trade and investment by the multinational corporations and support for sympathetic regimes which would protect the ideological and security interests of the United States, often at the expense of the native peoples. This goal has dictated a view of underdevelopment which is inconsistent with the realities of the Third World and its requirements for progressive change and development.

Development, whether in its political or economic sense, refers to that historical process by which societies have evolved from the primitive communities of the past to the industrial states of today. The term underdevelopment, therefore, is used to distinguish those societies which, at some stage in the developmental process, have fallen behind the societies whose *quantitative* progress remains uninterrupted. A principal misconception of the official U.S. view of underdevelopment has been the equation of quantitative development with the supposed qualitative superiority of U.S. values, habits and motivations.[8]

Of course satisfaction of basic human needs is a prerequisite for any qualitative change in the human condition, but such qualitative change does not follow automatically. Material growth can lead to a joyful existence and qualitative change only through people's conscious efforts and a systematic restructuring of the repressive and scarcity-oriented modes of thought and behavior which are committed to unending growth as a precondition for national security and prosperity. There is little indication that the established culture in the United States is going through any such process. And so long as the need for such a restructuring has entered the consciousness of only a very small and alienated segment of the population, the implicit contention of U.S. policymakers concerning the superiority of their values, habits and motivations over those of other societies should be viewed as lacking logic and evidence.[9]

It is due to this institutionalized ethnocentric conception of development that both the general public and most liberal students of politics and economics find it troubling to accept the view that noncapitalist methods of change and growth may be necessary and even humane, given the socio-economic conditions of underdeveloped societies. This ethnocentric attitude is so prevalent throughout U.S. society that the policymakers and their academic counterparts have no difficulty in equating capitalism with freedom and socialism with tyranny.

United States policymakers and their academic apologists often characterize underdeveloped nations as having a traditionally low per capita income, widespread illiteracy, a lack of political integration, a comparatively low degree of urbanization and industrialization, a lack of institutional continuity, a lack of national unity, particularism, functional diffuseness and so on. This characterization may be useful as a first step in describing the conditions of some underdeveloped societies. But if the above variables are analyzed in isolation, while disregarding the class structure of the society, the result will be a distorted picture of underdevelopment—and this distorted view is exactly what the official and semiofficial analysts have been perpetuating for the past twenty-five years.[10]

The reality of underdevelopment certainly includes the structural relations of all these usually named variables, but we must not forget that imperialism and class domination are the twin poles around which these other conditions revolve. It is impossible to have a meaningful conception of underdevelopment without considering class rule and imperialism as its mutually reinforcing beneficiaries and perpetuators.

The Truman Administration adopted the view that economic growth for the underdeveloped world could not occur until international stability was established and U.S. overseas economic interests were secure. In the late 1940s this meant the pressuring of noncolonial territories for new trade and investment and the intrusion of U.S. economic influence into the weakened colonial empires of France, Japan and Britain.[11]

The formula for this new wave of expansionism was symbolized in the Truman Doctrine. Through the use of crusading rhetoric President Truman justified the expenditure of $400 million in military and economic aid for Greece and Turkey by stating that "...it must be the policy of the U.S. to support free peoples who are resisting attempted subjugation by armed minorities or by outside pressures."[12] Here was the rationale for opposing the revolutionary movements in the underdeveloped world, a policy which in 1947 was primarily justified as a defense against Russian expansionism.

The Rio Conference in September of 1947 and the Inter-American Conference at Bogota in March of 1948 also emphasized the quest for international stability through collective security along with the protection of U.S. economic interests. The Bogota Conference was the source for the Investment Guaranty Program which insures U.S. citizens and corporations investing abroad against losses due to nationalization or the inability to convert income to U.S. dollars. By 1965 this program had been extended to over seventy underdeveloped countries receiving U.S. aid.[13]

In 1949 Truman's inaugural address called for a new governmental program, Point Four, to spread scientific and industrial knowledge to the Third World. The business community and Congress originally attacked the idea, demanding instead that Truman negotiate further treaties with underdeveloped nations assuring fair and equitable treatment for private investment and personnel.[14] Gradually, however, the Four Point program did become a key tool in the U.S. search for new markets and sources of raw materials.[15]

By early 1950 the U.S. concern for stability had turned to focus on Southeast Asia. Truman was in favor of large-scale aid for Bao Dai, and official State Department documents justified U.S. military and economic aid to France under the old rationale of blocking Soviet expansion.[16] But Truman's plan for stability in Indochina was linked to an overall program of military security for Southeast Asia in which Japan would play the dominant role. By September of 1951 John Foster Dulles and Secretary of State Acheson had negotiated a security treaty with Japan that allowed the stationing of U.S. troops and planes on its soil. The foundation was now built for the integration of

Southeast Asia into a world market system under U.S. control.[17] And so, by the advent of the Eisenhower years, the Truman policy of security prior to so-called economic development had resulted not only in a sizeable extension of U.S. economic and political influence, but also in the unquestioned acceptance by most U.S. citizens of such policies as moral and natural.

The inheritance of greater world hegemony produced a dilemma for the new Eisenhower Administration. Neither the Iranian crisis, the Guatemalan affair nor the Nasser coup were sufficient to convince Dulles that threats to U.S. economic interests in the underdeveloped world should not be expected to originate from open aggression by the Soviet armies.[18] Consequently, the Eisenhower Administration adopted the doctrine of massive retaliation at a time when the nature of new upheavals in Latin America, Asia and the Middle East rendered nuclear deterrence irrelevant.[19]

The misreading of the origins of the revolutionary situations in the underdeveloped world also heightened the contradictions in Eisenhower's economic doctrine. In his 1953 State of the Union message, President Eisenhower said that "a serious and explicit purpose of our foreign policy is the encouragement of a hospitable climate for investment in foreign nations."[20] This emphasis on private investment was supported by Secretary of the Treasury George Humphrey. In contradiction to the objectives of the U.S. foreign aid programs, the U.S. military posture had become one of massive retaliation which was incapable of coping with guerrilla warfare.

With the inauguration of J.F. Kennedy the style of rhetoric towards the underdeveloped world altered once again, as did the method of domination. On March 31, 1961, Kennedy stated, "Let us transform the American continent into a vast crucible of revolutionary ideas and efforts...an example to all the world that liberty and progress walk hand in hand. Let us once again awaken our American Revolution until it guides the struggles of people everywhere..."[24] In Latin America the vehicle for achieving this new freedom was to be bourgeois democratic reform supported by U.S. aid under the Alliance for Progress.

For those underdeveloped countries which chose more radical means based on the examples of the Cuban revolution or the ideology of the NLF, McNamara and Rostow supplemented a nuclear deterrence doctrine with a multidimensional military policy emphasizing counterinsurgency warfare.

But Kennedy's sophisticated verbiage was at most a tactical concession to democratic sentiment in the Third World. During the Kennedy years the U.S. supported every military coup in Latin America.[25] U.S. economic policy under Kennedy, while stressing government aid for economic development over direct private investment, made its AID loans repayable in dollars and raised the minimum loan rates to 2.5 percent, with Export-Import Bank and World Bank loans averaging 5.5 percent. As a consequence, debt servicing as a percentage of the recipient nation's income from foreign exports increased from 3.7 percent in 1956 to 9.1 percent by 1963, wiping out the advantages of loans to developing nations.[26] The objectives of the Kennedy Administration in the underdeveloped world were, in reality, consistent with those of Truman and Eisenhower—internal political and economic stabilization coordinated with intervention when necessary to preserve the status quo.

On April 26, 1966, President Johnson announced that U.S. foreign policy "...must always be an extension of our domestic policy. Our safest guide to what we do abroad is always what we do at home."[27] This statement made explicit what had been implicit in the foreign policy views of Truman, Eisenhower and Kennedy. It is domestic interests and ideological concerns rather than intentions and rhetoric which are the motivational forces behind U.S. foreign policy.[28] Two major events during the Johnson era serve to further document that fact, especially in relationship to the underdeveloped world.

In 1965, when the crisis in the Dominican Republic reached a point where the armed populace outnumbered the pro-Bosch military, there was a possibility of going beyond the type of middle class reforms which Kennedy had verbally supported in 1961.[29] It was at this point that the U.S. intervened because it was at this point that U.S. domestic financial and political interests were threatened. And in April of 1967 a military coup occurred in Greece with at least the tacit consent of the Johnson government. This coup was against the same liberal forces that had fought the communists in 1947, only this time, due to the lessening of the fear of Soviet military aggression and the centrifugal development in the world communist movement, there was no justification made of containing Soviet expansionism as there had been under Truman. However, in both 1947 and 1967 the interests which most benefitted from U.S. support were not those of the Greek people but rather those of U.S. companies such as ESSO, Reynolds Metal, Dow Chemical and Litton Industries, which since the stabilization of the Greek regime in the late 1940s have effectively gained control of large sections of the Greek economy.

By now it had become quite clear to many within the underdeveloped nations that there was no hope for development within the capitalist orbit. Development requires *both* economic and political change, and U.S. imperialism seemed to be hostile to the latter. While the sequence of economic development can be described as a "steady accumulation of wealth and a slow but growing expansion of income and employment,"[30] this strictly economic process "requires as a precondition the existence of a society in which wealth can be accumulated and in which incomes and employment are capable of being progressively enlarged."[31] The absence of this precondition in the new states makes the initial stages of economic development a social and political process. In many underdeveloped countries the force most antagonistic to the creation of these preconditions is the small privileged class which controls both the economic resources and the political institutions, including the instruments of coercion. The cooperation and mutual dependency between these privileged classes and the U.S. multinational corporations are well documented in the revisionist literature on United States foreign policy and underdevelopment.[32]

The interests of these ruling classes and those of the general population are so diametrically opposed that no modification or streamlining of the existing socio-economic system is likely to resolve their growing conflict.[33] Hence, the first step to end the inequitable distribution of wealth and power and thus create the precondition for socio-economic development is the destruction of class domination. This necessary feature of the developmental process is, by its very nature, antagonistic to both the short-run and long-run objectives of United States foreign policies. Inevitably, then, the policies of the United States toward underdeveloped countries in the 1970s favored support of reactionary military governments against actual or potential revolutionary challenge. These policies are also admissions of the long-standing fact that there exist in the Third World diverse national revolutionary forces dependent neither on Moscow nor Peking—forces much more threatening to U.S. hegemony than the "international communist conspiracy" which has embellished the rhetoric of U.S. views towards the underdeveloped world from Truman to Carter.

In the short run these revolutionary movements will not side with the United States in the cold war rivalry, nor will they favor perpetuation of the international status quo. They will not allow U.S. corporations to exploit their resources or turn their countries into a market for U.S. arms and surplus goods. In the long run successful revolutionary governments might restructure their societies in ways incompatible with the ideological and strategic goals of the United States. They might give material support to other revolutionary movements in the underdeveloped world and through the successful use of noncapitalist methods of development become a source of inspiration for other oppressed peoples. Such changes in the social structure and foreign relations of underdeveloped nations now in the U.S.-dominated camp can challenge the global ideological objectives of U.S. imperialism and jeopardize the economic and strategic interests of the capitalist world. The evolution and expansion of U.S. influence in the Middle East since the end of World War I is an instructive case. It shows how U.S. foreign policies have been adapted to the changing circumstances of the world in order to satisfy the strategic economic interests and the ideological objectives of U.S. imperialism.

Footnotes: Chapter 5

1. Garry Wills, *Nixon Agonistes* (New York: Signet, 1970), p. 429.
2. Ibid.
3. Ibid., p. 430.
4. Ibid.
5. Ibid., p. 421.
6. Ibid., p. 452.
7. Sources which help to document the nature of coporate influence on U.S. foreign policy are: G. William Domhoff, *Who Rules America?* (New Jersey: Englewood Cliffs, 1967); G. William Domhoff, "Where A Pluralist Goes Wrong," *Berkeley Journal of Sociology*, Vol. XIV (1969), pp. 35-38; David Horowitz, "Sinews of Empire," *Ramparts* (October 1969), pp. 32-42; Robert Engler, *The Politics of Oil* (New York: MacMillan, 1961); Gabriel Kolko, *The Roots of American Foreign Policy* (Boston: Beacon Press, 1969), especially the chapter on "The Men of Power."
8. See, for example, Truman's speech at Baylor University on 6 March 1947. Truman contended that the only way to peace and prosperity was the "American way." J.M. Jones, *The Fifteen Weeks* (New York: Harcourt, Brace, Jovanovich, Inc., 1965).
9. Herbert Marcuse, *One Dimensional Man* (Boston: Beacon Press, 1964); Jules Henry, *Culture Against Man* (New York: Random House, 1963).
10. Andre Gunder Frank, "Sociology of Development and Underdevelopment of Sociology," *Catalyst* (Summer 1977), pp. 20-73.
11. David Horowitz, *Empire and Revolution* (New York: Vintage, 1969), p. 91. In the initial postwar period the U.S. "inherited from Britain her spheres in Greece and the Middle East. From defeated Japan the U.S. openly seized Okinawa and her Pacific bases, while moving into a dominant position in South Korea and Taiwan; from France she secured Indochina...."
12. Harry Magdoff, *The Age of Imperialism* (New York: Monthly Review Press, 1969), pp. 127-128.
13. Walter LaFeber, *America, Russia, and the Cold War, 1945-1966* (New York: John Wiley and Sons, Inc., 1967), p. 73.
14. Gabriel Kolko, *The Roots of American Foreign Policy* (Boston: Beacon Press, 1967), p. 43.
15. Ibid., p. 44.
16. For a detailed analysis of the U.S. Pacific Rim strategy, see Peter Wiley, "Vietnam and the Pacific Rim Strategy," *Leviathan,* vol. 1, no. 3 (June 1969), and Jim Schoch, "Pacific Partnership," *Pacific*

Research and World Empire Telegram, vol. 3 (November-December 1969).

17. LaFeber, *Cold War*, p. 178.

18. Kolko, *American Foreign Policy*, p. 43.

19. Amaury de Riencourt, *The American Empire* (New York: Dell Publishing Co., 1968), pp. 133-134.

20. Raymond F. Midesell, *U.S. Private and Government Investment Abroad* (Eugene: University of Oregon, 1962), pp. 460-461.

21. Horowitz, *Empire and Revolution*, p. 224, footnote 5. "Under the Kennedy administration alone this included coups in El Salvador, Argentina, Peru, Guatemala and Ecuador."

22. Kolko, *American Foreign Power*, p. 92.

23. LaFeber, *Cold War*, p. 256.

24. For an excellent case study of this point see Fred Goff and Michael Locker, "The Violence of Domination: U.S. Power and the Dominican Republic," in T. Horowitz., *Latin American Radicalism* (New York: Vintage Paperbacks, 1969), pp. 249-291.

25. Horowitz, *Empire and Revolution*, pp. 227-228.

26. Robert L. Heilbroner, *The Great Ascent* (New York: Harper Torchbooks, 1963), p. 16.

27. Ibid.

28. Ibid.

29. Andre Gunder Frank, *Latin America: Underdevelopment or Revolution* (New York: Monthly Review Press, 1970); "The Underdevelopment Policy of the United States in Latin America," NACLA Newsletter, vol. II, no. 8 (December 1969).

30. John Gerassi, *The Great Fear in Latin America* (New York: Collier Books, 1967).

CHAPTER 6

THE U.S. IN THE MIDDLE EAST: A CASE STUDY

The purpose of the following analysis is to show how the development of U.S. policies toward the Middle East corresponds to the general patterns of U.S. imperialism as described in the previous chapters. An historian has used Poor Richard's famous proverb to characterize the attitudes of the United States toward the Mediterranean region. The proverb asserts, "An empty bag cannot stand upright." This means that "before the efforts of upright Americans to display their altruism through missionary and educational work could well begin, some progress had to be made toward filling the bag."[1]

The first motive for United States contact with the Mediterranean was commercial. The new American nation needed commercial connections to replace those lost by secession from the British Empire. These connections were developed by merchants and shipmasters, but they were not for long limited to a simple exchange of goods. The exchange of goods was soon followed by export of U.S. skills and missionary benevolence and a broadened perception of national interest.[2]

The loss of British protection created serious security problems for U.S. commercial navigation in the Mediterranean. In 1796 President Washington put it this way:

> from the best information I have been able to obtain, it would seem that our trade in the Mediterranean, without a protecting force, will always be insecure and our citizens exposed to calamities... These considerations invite the United States to look to the means, and to set out about the gradual creation of a Navy.[3]

In 1801 Thomas Jefferson committed this Navy to an undeclared war with Tripoli which lasted for four years. After winning this difficult war for the young republic, General William Easton "proclaimed to the Tripolians the American gospel of peace, trade, and prosperity."[4]

After this, with the exception of the temporary disruption caused by the War of 1812, early U.S. maritime activity enjoyed an open and tranquil Mediterranean. In some parts of the region U.S. rum was exchanged for what Henry Clay called an "invoice of figs and opium." The opium provided an important link in the early trade with China. This was the time when Indian opium was taking over the China market, when the opium war was underway, when John Quincy Adams was blasting the Chinese as anti-commercial and unchristian and regarding their refusal to get hooked on opium an outrage upon the rights of human nature.[5]

From the very beginning, the Mediterranean nations did not share the U.S. passion for trade. What they were interested in was U.S. skills. In the 1840s experts on cotton growing and salesmen for the Morse telegraph followed Samuel Colt and his revolvers to the Middle East. And they were all welcomed wherever they went. In this period U.S. missionary activity in the Middle East also enjoyed a steady growth, and missionaries established a number of pioneering schools and colleges throughout the region.

After the Civil War there was a significant increase in the U.S. shipment of manufactured goods to the Middle East, particularly armaments. In 1869 a sale of arms to Egypt was followed by a contingent of former officers under the leadership of General Charles P. Stone who, according to some historians, encouraged the abortive nationalist military coup of 1878 against the British. There were other U.S. exports to the Middle East in the 1870s. The most interesting of them all, retrospectively, was refined petroleum. In 1879 the U.S. Consul at Constantinople rejoiced in the fact that "even the sacred lamps over the Prophet's tomb at Mecca are fed with oil from Pennsylvania."[6] In the late 19th century the U.S. commercial presence in the Middle East diminished and U.S. political interest in the region remained marginal.

In the early 20th century both official and unofficial U.S. representation in the Middle East expanded. In 1909 the State Department set up a Division of Near Eastern Affairs. In 1911 the American Chamber of Commerce for the Middle East was established.

The first World War shattered the Ottoman Empire beyond repair. At the end of the war Woodrow Wilson's Fourteen Points raised the hopes of the colonized and oppressed throughout the Middle East. As one historian has noted, "In the Wilsonian program, missionaries saw hope for an Armenian nation, Iranians for support against both Russia and Great Britain, and Egyptians for freedom from the occupying power."[7] And the Jews saw the chance for creating their national home. The United States was held in such respect at the end of the war that there were some recommendations that the U.S. accept responsibility for the proposed subdivision of the Turkish Empire. But the United States was not yet ready.[8]

Between the two World Wars U.S. diplomacy in the Middle East emphasized the Open Door and equal opportunity for trade and investment. During this period U.S. economic, political and cultural interests in the region expanded rapidly. Also, in the interwar years, "the presence of the multinational corporation became increasingly evident, as cigarette and automobile manufacturers, branch banks, and oil companies followed the road earlier marked out by the Singer Sewing Machine."[9]

The interwar years also demonstrated the importance of petroleum to modern life. This recognition led to U.S. corporate diplomats becoming involved in the affairs of the Middle East long before the State Department did. Referring to the crisis of 1920, President Wilson wrote: "It is evident to me that we are on the eve of a commercial war of the severest sort and I am afraid that Great Britain will prove capable of as great a commercial savagery as Germany has displayed for so many years in her commercial methods."[10]

It was clear at the end of World War I that the British and U.S. interests were bound to clash in the Middle East. Wilson advocated the Open Door in the Middle East; the British opposed it because they had many concessions in the area and a physical presence to defend their interests.[11]

This period laid the foundation for the modern capitalist corporate state in the United States, and the oil industry was in the vanguard of this development. The major oil companies then became the chief and most visible advocates of a domestic need for foreign oil despite the discoveries of oil deposits in Texas, Louisiana and California. The resulting glut of crude oil did not change the major companies' moves to secure foreign reserves.[12]

In 1932, Gulf Oil secured the aid of the State Department in order to "open the door" in Bahrain and Kuwait. The British had earlier formally restricted the entry of non-British interests in Kuwait.[13] The U.S. ambassador in London was asked to obtain "equal treatment for American firms." This ambassador, coincidentally, was none other than Andrew Mellon, head of the Gulf empire, Secretary of the Treasury during the Teapot Dome scandal and the man responsible for securing the oil depletion allowance.[14]

In Saudi Arabia, U.S. companies did not have to enter into joint operation with the British. In 1932, Standard of California (Socal) was granted concessions for a period of sixty years covering most of eastern Saudi Arabia. The financial terms were five thousand francs per year until oil was discovered and royalties of four shillings a ton thereafter; a fifty thousand franc loan against these future royalties was offset by the King's agreement to forego for all time the right to tax the company. Oil was discovered in large quantities in 1938 and Socal's deal proved to be the world's richest oil concession. By the end of the 1930s the U.S. oil companies had obtained 42 percent of the known Middle East oil reserves.[15]

Until World War II U.S. policies toward the Middle East were intended to protect the commercial and missionary interest of U.S. citizens in the region with as little political involvement as possible. The region was regarded as an area of primarily European interest.

At the termination of the war the United States had a very different view of the region. During the war the U.S. played a significant part, both militarily and economically, in the British and Russian war efforts in the Middle East. The operation of the Lend-Lease Act in the region led to participation by the United States in the Middle East Supply Center. From 1942-1945 the U.S. Army was in charge of the Trans-Iranian Railway and controlled the southern parts of Iran in order to get urgently required material to the Russians at the Eastern Front. Those were the days when Radio Moscow referred to the U.S. troops in Iran as the angels of freedom.

During the war it became clear that the importance of oil as a source of energy was going to increase beyond all expectations. Before the war was over this recognition led to competition between the U.S. and the British for Middle Eastern oil. At that time the British were in control of the oil resources of Iran and Iraq. The U.S. controlled the deposits in Saudi Arabia. Competition between the British and the U.S. reached "the Roosevelt-Churchill level," with Roosevelt remarking to Churchill that he was disturbed by "the rumor that the British wish to horn in on Saudi Arabian oil reserves," and with Churchill replying that he was glad to hear that the Americans were not casting "sheep's eyes" on British oil fields in Iran and Iraq and saying he wished to give "the fullest assurances that we have no thought of trying to horn in upon your interests or property in Saudi Arabia."[16]

At the end of World War II, then, all the big oil players were on the scene. The "seven sisters," as they were later dubbed, were locked into joint production and marketing arrangements without significant competition. United States strategy in the post-World War II Middle East is summarized in a memorandum from Navy Secretary Forrestal to the Secretary of State issued in 1944:

> It is distinctly in the strategic interest of the United States to encourage industry to promote the orderly development of petroleum reserves in the more remote areas such as the Persian Gulf, thereby supplementing the Western Hemisphere sources and protecting against their early exhaustion... The prestige and hence the influence of the United States is in part related to the wealth of the Government and its nationals in terms of oil resources, foreign as well as domestic... The bargaining power of the United States in international conferences involving vital materials like oil and such problems as aviation, shipping, island bases, and international security agreements relating to the disposition of armed forces and facilities, will depend in some degree upon the retention by the United States of such oil resources... Under these circumstances it is patently in the Navy's interest that no part of the national wealth, as represented by the present holdings of foreign oil reserves by American nationals, be lost at this time. Indeed, the active expansion of such holdings is very much to be desired.[17]

U.S. policy during and after the war was to replace the British economically but to support a British military presence in Greece, Iraq, Jordan and Libya. U.S. strategists assumed that the British would maintain a substantial enough economic interest in Middle Eastern oil to keep a British military presence in the area.

The post-World War II National Front movement in Iran and the nationalization of the Iranian oil industry created the first scene of outright competition. The National Front was an anti-imperialist coalition of a number of small political parties, religious leaders and the liberal leftist intelligentsia. Dr. Mohammad Mossadeq was the unchallenged leader of this coalition. The unifying objective of the National Front was to nationalize the Anglo-Iranian oil company and end British interference in the affairs of the country. The Tudeh (the Communist Party of Iran) was against the nationalization proposal because the Soviet Union was seeking to secure oil concessions in northern Iran. From the very beginning of the post-World War II nationalist movement, the Tudeh, echoing the Soviet line, opposed the National Front objectives and portrayed the ideologically diverse National Front leaders as dupes or agents of United States imperialism.[18]

During World War II, the Iranian army had been aided by United States advisors and later was provided with equipment and training. Having already entered the Iranian scene, the United States steered the National Front forces against the British while continuing to support the Shah and the army. The real competitor of the United States in post-World War II Iran was not the Soviet Union or communism, but Great Britain. The strategy of the United States in the Iranian crisis was to replace the British as the dominant foreign power in the country. This new imperialist rivalry in Iran was a principal factor shaping the development of Iranian politics in the post-World War II period. The new constellation of power severely limited British and Russian options in dealing with this phase of Iranian nationalism.

Following the overthrow of Mossadeq by the CIA-sponsored coup d'etat in August, 1953, an agreement was reached between the Shah and the oil companies giving Iran nominal sovereignty over the oil fields while vesting management and commercial rights in a consortium of oil companies. British Petroleum took 40 percent interest; five major U.S. oil companies took 40 percent; and the rest went to eight small U.S. oil companies.[19] Thus, in the age of oil as in the age of figs and opium, commercial expansion was the pathfinder of the U.S. secular mission.

The Truman Doctrine provided the ideological basis for the deepening U.S. political involvement in the Middle East.

The Truman Doctrine had two interrelated objectives: 1) to contain the revolutionary or potentially revolutionary movements in the underdeveloped world; and 2) to maintain order and stability within the traditionally class-oriented societies.[20] In reality, preserving order in the Middle Eastern societies during the post-World War II period meant suppressing those forces which challenged the existing political structures; it meant, in effect, maintenance of the repressive status quo in the name of protection from a more repressive alternative, namely the presumed communist aggression. President Truman might be credited with "saving" Greece and Turkey, but the logic of his Doctrine was based on the proposition that the economic, military, political and ideological objectives of the U.S. could best be served by the status quo situation. Thus the fear of communist aggression, which was genuinely felt by many, was also a useful rationale to make imperialistic expansion look both moral and necessary.

Truman's support for the establishment of the State of Israel was another step involving the U.S. in the affairs of the Middle East. Starting with Woodrow Wilson, every U.S. President gave his vague general support for a Jewish national home in Palestine. During the 1920s and 1930s Jewish elements in the U.S. exerted some pressure on the U.S. government to take a more active role in establishing this state. Such a position made good sense in certain areas of the U.S. for electoral purposes, but it did not make sense for U.S. interests in the Middle East. So U.S. policymakers stayed on the sideline and left the headache to the British. Then came World War II and the systematic annihilation of millions of Jews. This led most countries of the world to support the creation of a Jewish state in Palestine.

The significant thing about the U.S. decision to support the establishment of the State of Israel was that at the time it ran against the growing economic interests of the United States in the Arab world. This is why from 1945-1948 the White House and not the State Department was in charge of U.S. Palestinian policy. President Truman once remarked to a group of U.S. diplomats in the Middle East that he had many Zionist supporters among his constituents, but not many Arab constituents.[21]

United States Middle East policy in the immediate post-World War II period was one of those "rare cases where strategic interests as defined by the national security managers, commercial interests as defined by the major corporations operating in the area, and domestic political interests as defined by those in the business of winning elections did not neatly coincide."[22] After the establishment of Israel the U.S. followed a policy of trying to work with both sides to reduce tension in the area. This meant preserving the status quo and calling it even-handedness.

Eisenhower and Dulles, like Truman and Acheson, saw every upheaval in the Middle East as a localized testing of the United States' will to resist Soviet aggression. But Dulles was critical of Truman policies, labelling them piecemeal. "They cannot be depended upon to serve our long-time interests ... Our purpose is to make these relations more effective, less costly. This can be done by placing more reliance on deterrent power and less dependence on local defensive power ..."[23] Consequently the Eisenhower Administration adopted the doctrine of massive retaliation at a time when the nature of new upheavals in the Middle East rendered nuclear deterrence irrelevant.

Thus, the Truman Doctrine was replaced in 1956 by a somewhat more sophisticated rationale, the Eisenhower Doctrine. The initial $200 million authorization for military and economic aid under this new policy was intended to protect U.S. oil interests in the Middle East. The dispatch of the Sixth Fleet to the Mediterranean to protect King Hussein of Jordan and the landing of troops in Lebanon in 1958 were justified as safeguarding the preservation of the independence and integrity of the nations of the Middle East.[24] In this way the rhetoric of opposition to aggression, so prevalent under Truman, slowly gave way under Eisenhower to a call for independence and integrity for nations of the Middle East. Both policies, however, were intended to contain internal radical change and protect the United States' expanding political power and economic interests in the region.

John Foster Dulles stressed the regional security pact as a way of preserving the status quo in the Middle East. The

Baghdad Pact or, as it has been known since early 1959, the Central Treaty Organization, was supposed to serve this purpose. Iraq, Turkey, Iran, Pakistan and Great Britain were the formal member nations. The United States was a member in substance but not in name. Dulles considered this pact as part of a "worldwide warning system" and a major gain "for the system of collective security."[25]

After the collapse of Iraq's semifeudal kingdom in 1958 and the subsequent withdrawal of Iraq from the CTO, the United States signed three identical agreements with Iran, Pakistan and Turkey. In these agreements the U.S. affirmed that it would continue to furnish military and economic assistance to all three countries in order to help them preserve the status quo.

U.S. intervention in the Lebanese crisis of 1958 is an interesting example of how the Eisenhower Administration perceived the internal politics of the Middle Eastern countries. In 1958, President Chamoun of Lebanon was challenged by two growing forces in Lebanese politics. First, the Moslems, due to high birth rate and immigration from Palestine, were fast turning into a majority. The Christians viewed this as a threat to their privileged position. Second, Nasser's call for Arab unity was finding converts in Lebanon. Beirut had always been a center of Arab integrationist thought. Nasser politicized this ideal after the Suez crisis of 1956. An Arab wresting of the Suez Canal from the British Empire aroused feelings of pride among Arabs everywhere.

Lebanese Christians had committed themselves in the National Pact not to make alliances with the West. But President Chamoun, who had refused to join the Baghdad Pact four years earlier, now moved to line up with the U.S. Cold Warriors as a way of maintaining the rule of his faction of the Maronites. The consequences of Chamoun's decision were a massive political crisis and the subsequent civil war in 1958. President Chamoun ordered the army to put down the rebellion, but General Faud Shehab, the commander-in-chief, refused the order and contended that the rebellion was a mass protest rather than subversion. On July 4, 1958, President Chamoun sent

President Eisenhower an urgent telegram requesting the landing of U.S. troops in his country. Eisenhower dispatched 14,000 Marines, twice the size of the Lebanese army, and sent Robert Murphy, a veteran diplomat, to Lebanon to evaluate the situation. Murphy quickly realized that Chamoun could not be saved. He then contacted the rebels and announced the U.S. abandonment of Chamoun. On July 31 General Shehab was elected President and the fighting died away. By October of the same year the Marines left Lebanon without having fired a single shot. The irony of the U.S. involvement is that the Marines went in to protect President Chamoun and they ended up sacrificing him for a negotiated settlement.

The Kennedy and Johnson administrations did not make any change in the Middle East strategy of U.S. foreign policy. However, the Nixon Doctrine of creating outposts of U.S. military power in the Middle East led to a significant modification of U.S. strategy in the region. These changes were greatly influenced by the collapse of U.S. efforts in Vietnam, the unexpected developments in Egypt after the death of Nasser and the Arab-Israeli War of 1973. The development of United States policies toward the Arab-Israeli conflict and Iran concretely illustrates the imperialistic character of U.S. objectives in the region.

United States Strategy In The Arab-Israeli Conflict

To understand U.S. strategy in the Arab-Israeli conflict, it is necessary to keep in mind that the Arab states do not have a common policy toward Israel. Each state pursues its exclusive national objectives, sometimes at the expense of others. Arab unity is a hope or a dream to advocate in public lectures but not a real objective in any nation's policy. Expressions of concern for the plight of Palestinians are often in the same category. All the confrontation states have abused and oppressed the Palestinians at one time or another since their emergence as a political force following the 1967 war. Jordan slaughtered and expelled thousands of them in 1970. In the Lebanese civil war an estimated 40,000 Palestinians were killed, many of them by Syrian forces. Egypt has never allowed them to have any significant activity inside its territory.

Petrodollars belong to "the Arabs" in the same way that Wall Street assets belong to "New Yorkers." The vast majority of the forty million Egyptians, three million Jordanians, eight million Syrians and three million Lebanese are among the most impoverished people of the world. The Saudi and Kuwaiti rulers have as much actual concern for the poor Arabs as the directors of the Stock Exchange and Chase Manhattan have for the residents of Harlem.

United States interests in the Middle East have been growing exponentially during the past five years. Oil, as the lifeblood of the industrial world, has become more important than ever before. Thus, order and stability in the Middle East have also become more important than ever before. Any extended interruption in the flow of oil from the region could paralyze the industrial world. The increase in the price of oil has made the Middle East more important as a market for United States' products than ever before. This increase in U.S. exports helps dampen the growing deficit in the balance of trade—a deficit in part created by the heavy reliance of the U.S. on imported oil.

The importance of the Middle East as a market coincides with a growing competition among the industrial countries for foreign markets. The U.S. exporters of arms, military knowledge, machinery and consumer goods do not want to lose customers to Russia, France, England, Germany and Japan. Thus, congenial relations between the United States and the oil rich countries have become more important than ever before. The key to achieving this objective is to help the "moderate" elites against the actual or potential radical nationalist forces in the region. The requirements of law and order as perceived by the feudal sheiks and the traditionalist tyrants of the region coincide with what the United States regards as essential to its interests. Thus, what has developed in the Middle East, both politically and economically, is a congruence or convergence of interests, values and attitudes between the conservative forces in the region and U.S. foreign policy makers.

The strategy of using the Arab-Israeli conflict as an instrument of U.S. foreign policy in the region seems to be moving in the expected direction. The Carter administration continued the Nixon-Kissinger strategy without substantive modification. This strategy has three interrelated objectives: 1) Israel should remain a military power vastly superior to the Arab states; 2) Egypt has to be a *status quo* state and dependent on the United States; and 3) the radical nationalistic elements, including the PLO, are to be isolated and put on the defensive.

As for the first objective of this strategy, it suffices to say that between 1970 and 1978 the United States gave Israel $15 billion of military aid, credit sales and grants, more than fifty times the previous twenty years' total.[26] Indeed, in fiscal year 1981, of about $3.4 billion in foreign assistance almost $800 million went to Israel. Thus, almost 25% of all foreign aid went to a country with a per capita GNP approximately matching such European countries as Ireland, Italy and Spain, and nearly matching that of England. This quantitative increase has been coupled with a very liberal attitude concerning the quality and variety of weapons that the Israelis can receive. Today Israel has reached the peak of its military might in both absolute and relative terms.[27]

To pursue the second objective of the strategy, the United States needed not just cooperation from Anwar Sadat but collaboration. Nasser was a rare Arab leader who simultaneously embodied nationalism, populism and socialism. The men who served under him had diverse political beliefs but their differences had no political significance so long as Nasser was in command. After Nasser's sudden death in 1970, there was a power struggle among these men. This struggle was not limited to the possession of power per se but also was waged over the economic, military and ideological goals of the country. Anwar Sadat emerged victorious in the power struggle among the Egyptian military elites and in the process substantially moved the leadership in a conservative direction. For example, in February, 1971 President Sadat directed his government to return the expropriated land of 800 wealthy Egyptian families. He ended the Egyptian call for Arab unity and established a close relationship with King Faisal of Saudi Arabia, who visited Egypt in June, 1971.

In all these decisions he sharply departed from Nasser's policies. Nasser was a passionate proponent of Arab unity and socialist strategy for economic development. He regarded the government of Saudi Arabia as the most reactionary regime in the region. The elimination of Ali Sabri, leader of the pro-Soviet Nasserites, on May 2, 1971, the day before William Rogers arrived in Cairo, was a prelude to the expulsion of the Soviet military experts in July of 1972. President Sadat tried to show Secretary Rogers that Egypt was interested in establishing close relations with the United States on both economic and military terms.[28]

Sadat's aim in launching the October 1973 war was primarily to open up political possibilities by breaking the stalemate in the Arab-Israeli confrontation. The conservative Arab states were feeling threatened by Israeli military power, and their support for Egypt and Syria was an effort to pressure the United States into containing Israel. As Eqbal Ahmad has stated in his analysis of the October War and subsequent developments,

> The October War ended the complacency with which Washington had regarded the stalemate. It destroyed the assumption of Arab equanimity in accepting protracted occupation and of their incompetence in war. It demonstrated Israel's power as too derivative to be totally dependable. The oil embargo underscored the dependence of Japanese and European (and to a lesser extent American) economies on Arab oil, dramatized the contradictions in Atlantic relations and underlined the importance of the Middle East in perpetuating America's global predominance ... Under the circumstances Kissinger's bid to act as the mediator was inevitable. Given the objectives which motivated Egyptian recourse to war and conservative Arab support for it, President Sadat's capitulation to Kissinger's blue-print for peacemaking was equally predictable.[29]

Sadat's capitulation was not limited to Egypt's role in the Arab-Israeli conflict. In February, 1974, Sadat announced a new economic policy which offered broader guarantees on investments and greater protection against nationalization. Enterprises investing in the Canal Free Zones were to be exempt from taxes and duties. In the rest of Egypt, new enterprises would not be required to pay any tax on profits for a period of five to eight years. In June, 1974, an investment law was passed which admitted foreign investors into Egyptian industry, banking and insurance, all of which had been previously nationalized. Another law was passed at the same time allowing Egyptian nationals to represent foreign firms, effectively destroying the public sector's control of the import trade. Thus the new economic policy, which was appropriately labeled "open door" by the Egyptian government, resulted in the public sector serving the interests of domestic and international capital. The policy was aimed at creating a capitalist form of economic stimulation based on profit and competition. The combined effects of the open door policy made impossible any economic planning that restricted the freedom of private capital.[30]

The change in Egyptian domestic and foreign policies was from the very beginning encouraged and rewarded by the United States. U.S. mediation in regaining Egyptian territory in the Sinai has been augmented by an annual $800 million in economic aid since 1973.[31] Saudi Arabia has also rewarded Sadat for departing from the radical nationalism of Nasser.[32]

Thus, U.S. strategists were not unrealistic in perceiving Sadat as a collaborator in the implementation of their strategy in the Arab-Israeli conflict. Henry Kisinger's step-by-step diplomacy and the two Sinai agreements were the prelude to the meeting of Sadat and Begin in Tel Aviv. And, as President Carter expected, the Camp David summit led to a peace agreement between Egypt and Israel which was intended to isolate the PLO, neutralize Syria and keep Israel as the most feared and least challenged military power in the region. The United States helped Sadat to regain the formal prerogative of Egyptian sovereignty over the Sinai, but the Sinai seemed likely to remain demilitarized so long as Egypt had no actual power to enforce her territorial sovereignty.

As the most populous country in the Middle East, Egypt in the 1970s has become a very important ally of the United States.

In its foreign policy, Egypt has acted against the Soviet interests in the region. It has changed the regional equation of ideological and power relations in favor of the conservative forces. In its domestic policy, Egypt has abandoned the path of Nasserite socialism and adopted a capitalistic strategy for development. The United States will do everything in its power to preserve the conservative forces in Egypt, but the way this objective has to be pursued is more complicated than it seems to be.

The shift to the right in Egypt was the product of a personal preference, not the exercise of institutionalized ideology. In Egypt, as in the rest of the Arab world, there is no institutional continuity or peaceful succession of authority. Just as Anwar Sadat could reverse eighteen years of Nasserite socialism in three years, another military man could do the same thing to Sadat's domestic and foreign policies. Thus, the United States cannot count on the continuation of the Egyptian government's present ideological orientation when Sadat leaves the scene, voluntarily or otherwise. Therefore, it is the institutional continuity and the military might of Israel that the United States will have to rely on in pursuit of its economic, strategic and ideological interests in the region.

On June 26, 1970, in a background briefing at San Clemente, Henry Kissinger said, "We are trying to get a Middle East settlement in such a way that the moderate regimes are strengthened, and not the radical regimes."[33] On December 28, 1977, in a television interview, President Carter said, "Permanent peace can best be maintained if there is not a fairly radical, new independent nation in the heart of the Middle Eastern area." In the lexicon of U.S. foreign policy makers, "moderate" or "not fairly radical" means regimes like those in Jordan, Saudi Arabia and Sadat's Egypt. To be moderate means to side with the United States in conflict situations, buy weapons from U.S. arms manufacturers, keep the country open to multinational corporations, be anticommunist and pursue a capitalist strategy for economic development.

If the purpose of the U.S.-sponsored peace agreement between Egypt and Israel is to strengthen such regimes, then any peace settlement that can lead to the creation or strengthening of nonmoderate regimes is a threat to U.S. interests in the region. From this perspective, peace between Israel and her neighbors is an instrument of U.S. foreign policy, and not a valued objective in and of itself. Thus, if Washington finds an absence of peace to be more suitable to U.S. strategy, it will prefer conflict to peace, as it did before the shift to the right in Egypt.

This shift will logically lead to the Americanization of the Egyptian army. The Pentagon cannot penetrate the Egyptian armed forces unless the Russian weapons are replaced with U.S. weapons. This has to be done gradually because the stability of the present Egyptian government is more precarious than what is portrayed by Sadat's showmanship. Thus the sale of 50 F-5E's to Egypt is the first step in the process of transforming Egypt's Russian-equipped army to an U.S.-equipped army. Reporting the problems caused by the speed of U.S. aid to Egypt, the Washington Post correspondent writes from Cairo,

> The stackup of unspent funds has reached about $1.9 billion, excluding another $1.5 billion in military aid and $300 million in extra economic aid decided this spring as part of President Carter's bargain with Israel and Egypt that helped persuade them to sign the treaty.... Overall, the United States has pledged more than $3.7 billion in economic assistance to Egypt between 1975 and the end of last month.[35]

The Israelis do not view their peace treaty of March, 1979, with Egypt as a comprehensive resolution of the conflict with Arab Palestinians, but rather as a blow to the ability of the Palestinians to introduce their moral claim to the debate surrounding the security of Israel. Like other Israeli foreign policy strategists, Begin believes that when Egypt is effectively neutralized Syria will not be able to fight alone and the Palestinian demand for a national homeland will become a manageable nuisance. He is adamantly committed to the indefinite continuation of Israeli military rule in the West Bank and the Gaza along with the establishment of more settlements and the official annexation of Jerusalem.[34]

The Israelis and their supporters in the Western mass media often use the sensational violence of the Palestinians in order to portray them as terrorists and thus irrational and heartless. What they fail to remember is that the poor have always used less sophisticated means of killing their enemies than the rich. The violence of the poor usually involves direct personal contact with the enemy. The reverse is true for the rich. Technology has vastly increased the ability of the rich to remain detached from the objects of their violence. The indiscriminate bombing of the Palestinians in their refugee camps is considered a combat action in defense of Israeli territory, while hijacking or kidnapping by the Palestinians is considered an act of simple terrorism. This inequality of means enables the Israelis to distort the reality of their actions and intention, and they have the media to continually perpetuate this distortion. One can hold the Palestinians as much responsible for what they do to their victims as the Israelis, but one cannot differentiate the violence of the two in favor of Israel without engaging in sophistry.

A complicating factor in all this is that many observers, including Anwar Sadat and his "moderate" Arab friends, are of the mistaken opinion that U.S. support for Israel is a product of American Jewish pressure on the United States' government. It is true that American Jews significantly influenced the decision of the United States government to aid the creation of the Zionist state. It is also true that American Jews influence the tactics of the United States in the Arab-Israeli conflict. But the continuity of U.S. support for Israel and the generous economic assistance given to it for thirty years must be understood in the context of U.S. objectives in the region.

Since World War II United States policies in the Middle East have been committed to the following goals: 1) to keep the region in the capitalist orbit; 2) to control the region for strategic and geopolitical purposes; 3) to contain the ongoing revolutionary challenge to the "moderate" power structures; 4) to protect and expand the interests of the United States oil companies; and 5) to prevent, minimize or eliminate Soviet political and military influence in the region. As demonstrated in this analysis, the military strength of Israel is designed to be a part of the U.S. strategy in the region.

The irony is that from 1948 to 1967 the United States ignored the Arab Palestinians politically, while contributing more than any other nation to their sustenance in the refugee camps. But once the Palestinians became an effective political force following the 1967 war, the United States began to view them as a threat to its interests. Even so, after 1967, four Presidents and numerous other political and religious leaders have confessed the essential truth of the Palestinian claim against Israel.[36] Despite these admissions, the Palestinians, as the most oppressed and thus the least "moderate" protagonist in the dispute, were destined to be opposed by U.S. imperialism.[37]

As the most oppressed and abused people in the Middle East since World War II, the Palestinians were bound to become radical in their perception of Israel as their enemy. General Moshe Dayan has spoken quite clearly of the Palestinian predicament. "It is not true that the Arabs hate the Jews for personal, religious, or racial reasons. They consider us—and justly, from their point of view—as Westerners, foreigners, invaders who have seized an Arab country to turn it into a Jewish state."[38] Again, speaking at a funeral of a murdered friend, Dayan said, "We must beware of blaming the murderers. Who are we to reproach them for hating us? Colonists who transform into Jewish homeland the territory they have lived in for generations."[39]

Since 1948, almost all Arab governments have used the plight of the Palestinians for propaganda purposes without doing much to change their conditions. The Israelis, with generous help from the U.S. media, usually attempt to equate the condemnation of Israeli policies toward Arab Palestinians with support for Arab governments.[40] They try to confuse the claims of the Palestinians with the demagoguery of Arab politicians. This Israeli method of distorting the reality of the Palestinian plight is consistent with the pattern of U.S. imperialist attitudes toward the wretched of the earth.

Iran And The Nixon Doctrine

After the departure of Shah Mohammed Reza Pahlavi from Iran in January, 1979, U.S. foreign policy makers were forced to ask themselves several disturbing questions. What had happened in Iran, and why? How could most U.S. government officials have believed, even as late as the fall of 1978, that the Shah had the overwhelming support of his people? Why did the U.S. equate Iranian stability with the coercive power of the Shah? Had the U.S. intelligence community been primarily responsible for U.S. failure to perceive the fragility of the Shah's regime and the depth and strength of the Iranian opposition?[41] Such apparent soulsearching on the part of U.S. policymakers cannot lead to a realistic assessment of the developing situation in Iran simply because imperialists are not capable of investigating their own actions objectively.

The U.S.-Iranian relationship since World War II provides a prototypical example of U.S. imperialism as a transnational system of privilege. What U.S. officials failed to perceive above all else was that the intense anti-American character of the Iranian revolution was the logical outgrowth of more than 30 years of U.S. policy toward Iran. The consistent U.S. treatment of Iran as a client state in the postwar period involved a primary emphasis on maintaining the Shah's dictatorial regime. Preserving the Iranian status quo required severe internal repression. The militarization of the Iranian state, and the intrusion of the SAVAK into all aspects of daily life were structural byproducts of the imperialist relationship.

At the onset of the cold war, U.S. policymakers perceived opposition to existing regimes as evidence of Soviet-backed communist aggression. Therefore, the maintenance of a repressive status quo was justified by the presumed need to prevent an even more repressive alternative, namely Soviet expansionism. Iran, because of the border it shares with the Soviet Union, was considered a prime site for practical application of the Truman Doctrine.

> Though the Red Army withdrew from Azerbaijan, pressure from Moscow has not abated—these are signs that it is increasing.

> Iran is in the midst of the cold war.... It is not in the United States' interest that Iran should disappear behind the Iron curtain...
>
> Iran needs an army capable primarily of maintaining order within the country, an army capable of putting down any insurrection—no matter where or by whom inspired or abetted... It will encourage Iran in the maintenance of her present position as a free and independent country. It is definitely in the U.S. interest.[42]

Thus, at the outset, the U.S. committed itself to upholding the status quo in Iran. Any threats to the existing regime were to be countered with the military instrument. The Iranian army was to be strengthened with U.S. aid so that its power would be sufficient to resist both internal opposition and expected pressure from Moscow. U.S. fear of communist aggression provided a useful rationale for imperialist expansion, making U.S. policies appear both moral and necessary. Although the real competitor of the U.S. in post-World War II Iran was not the Soviet Union or communism, but Great Britain, as we saw in the previous section, the U.S. used the superpower confrontation to justify deeper involvement in Iranian affairs. Furthermore, the Iranian military became the primary instrument through which the U.S. pursued its policy objectives in the country.

The competition between England and the U.S. for control of Iranian oil did not surface until the early 1950s, when the Iranian National Front government led by Dr. Mohammed Mossadeq voted to nationalize the Iranian oil industry in hopes of ending British interference in Iran. Both nationalization and the National Front enjoyed widespread popularity in the country. U.S. strategy, which aimed at replacing the British as the dominant economic and political power in Iran, steered the National Front forces against the British while continuing to support the Shah and the army. When, in 1953, it became apparent that an oil agreement favorable to U.S. interests was not forthcoming, a CIA-sponsored coup d'etat deposed Mossadeq and restored the Shah to power. U.S. policymakers justified the intervention on the grounds that economic and political chaos in Iran threatened to produce a communist takeover of the government.[43]

In terms of long-run consequences for U.S.-Iranian relations, the 1953 coup marks a turning point. The years 1951-53 are still viewed by Iranians as a period of national triumph and a source of national pride. The U.S. role in ending what many regard as the only postwar interlude of genuine political freedom in Iran cemented the link between perceived U.S. national interest and the fate of the Shah. Increased U.S. military aid became the means whereby the Shah bolstered the Iranian military and the secret police, and these in turn were the principal means by which he maintained an increasingly repressive rule. The Baghdad Pact (Central Treaty Organization) was designed to serve this repressive purpose. This pact made the Shah somewhat uneasy, and he voiced further complaints that the political crisis of 1951-53 could have been averted if adequate financial assistance from the U.S. had been forthcoming in the immediate postwar years. Consequently, in 1959, the U.S. signed a bilateral security agreement with Iran, reinforcing its commitment to provide military and economic assistance to preserve the Shah's regime.[44]

Increasing political disaffection to Pahlavi rule was virtually ignored by U.S. officials. The United States equated Iran's stability with the Shah's capacity to keep the lid on dissent. The opposition was viewed by U.S. officials, as well as by the Shah, as more of an embarrassment than an actual threat to his rule.[45] There is no reason, given the logic of U.S. imperialism, that one should expect otherwise. United States support for the Iranian army and secret police created effective instruments of repression. And the Shah's will to utilize these instruments coincided neatly with the U.S. desire to suppress opposition to *status quo* regimes. The fact that the Pahlavi rule lacked any significant base of popular support consistently escaped the grasp of U.S. policymakers.

The Kennedy and Johnson administrations did not alter the basic U.S. posture toward Iran. However, the Nixon Doctrine of creating regional outposts of U.S. military power led to a significant modification of U.S. strategy. Local armies in sensitive areas of the world were to be furnished with conventional U.S. arms and trained by U.S. personnel as part of a global counter-revolutionary strategy.[46]

President Nixon announced this new policy of the United States toward Asia informally on Guam in July, 1969. The Doctrine, as expressed by Nixon, lacked precise meaning. He later claimed that the Doctrine was supposed to initiate a dialogue between the United States and the world, "To attempt to define the new diplomacy completely by ourselves would repeat the now presumptuous instinct of the previous era and violate the very spirit of our new approach."[47] Contrary to this claim, the President's often quoted words from his first State of the World address contain the general parameters of his Doctrine,

> First, the United States will keep all of its treaty commitments. Second, we shall provide a shield if a nuclear power threatens the freedom of a nation allied with us, or of a nation whose survival we consider vital to our security. Third, in cases involving other types of aggression we shall furnish military and economic assistance when requested in accordance with our treaty commitments. But we shall look to the nation directly threatened to assume the primary responsibility of providing the manpower for its defense.[48]

The Nixon Doctrine was the outcome of the U.S. failure in Vietnam but it was intended to pursue the same counter-revolutionary policy that brought about the direct military involvement of the United States in the Indochina war. Mao Tse Tung once described the guerrilla as a fish and the countryside as the sea. The U.S. strategists in Vietnam, in their attempt to protect the peasants from the influence of the Vietcong guerrillas, decided to dry out the sea in order to starve the fish. To achieve this objective, many Vietnamese villages were destroyed and the countryside defoliated.[49] Along with the use of such coercive means, U.S. troops were charged with the task of persuading Vietnamese peasants to leave their villages. When this method of defeating or containing the Vietnamese revolution failed, policymakers in Washington formulated the policy of Vietnamization to pursue the same objective.

However, Vietnamization was not just a policy in the Indochina war, but rather it was the beginning of a new phase in the global counter-revolutionary strategy of the United States. It was this larger meaning of Vietnamization which became the essence of the Nixon Doctrine. David Packard, President Nixon's deputy secretary of defense, explained the Nixon Doctrine in 1970 in the following words,

> The best hope of reducing our overseas involvements and expenditures lies in getting allied and friendly nations to do even more in their own defense. To realize that hope, however, requires that we must continue, if requested, to give or sell them the tools they need for this bigger load we are urging them to assume.[50]

Two domestic groups welcomed the Nixon Doctrine the most—politicians and arms manufacturers. The politicians wanted to extricate U.S. troops because their constituencies could not stand the heavy casualties; the arms manufacturers were badly in need of foreign orders.

Thus, as a concept, Vietnamization meant training and equipping local armies in the sensitive areas of the world in order to create outposts of U.S. power. Iran was an excellent candidate for one of the outposts. The Shah was a proven friend of the United States and his strategically important country was perceived as the most stable in the region. Furthermore, in 1968, Britain, due to economic difficulties, had decided to speed up the already planned withdrawal of its forces from the Persian Gulf. This action, official Washington believed, was creating a "vacuum of power" in the region, which had to be filled either by the United States itself or a powerful ally.[51] Iran was certainly an ally but not sufficiently powerful. However, it had the potential to become powerful with its 35 million people and the fourth largest oil reserve in the world. In addition, nothing could delight the Shah of Iran more than possessing sophisticated weapons and playing the king of kings (or deputy sheriff of the United States) in the Gulf region. To complete the setting for the largest arms sales in history, Nixon and Kissinger visited the Shah in Tehran on their way back from Moscow in May, 1972. In their historic meeting "...the Shah stressed to Nixon that Russian Foxbats (MiG 25s) had been flying over Iranian soil, and insisted he must have the most up-to-date fighters. Nixon agreed to sell Iran 'virtually any conventional arms it wanted,' supported by unlimited U.S. technicians in Iran; and he personally told the Shah that he could choose between the two new-generation planes, the Tomcat and the Eagle."[52] Needless to say, the $20 billion U.S. arms sale to Iran between 1972 and 1977 would not have been possible without a substantial increase of oil prices during the same period.

The decision to transform Iran into an outpost of U.S. power was mutually satisfactory to the Shah and to the United States. Neither side imposed itself on the other; they both acted without any regard for the best interests of the Iranian people. The Shah simply believed that "he was born to be a king, that his legitimacy was rooted in the supernatural, that he was the embodiment of the divine law, and thus beyond criticism."[53] And the United States believed that the Shah was loved by his people and that Iranians who opposed him did not have the capacity to be more than troublesome.[54] The essence of the Shah's regional role, as Richard Falk has written, "was to build a Middle East alliance of reactionary forces in the region to contain radical challenges and to undergird the security of Israel. The Egyptian-Israel accord must be understood as the latest episode in that strategic quest."[55] This objective was acknowledged by the Senate report on the "special relationship" between Iran and the United States,

> If Iran is called upon to intervene in the internal affairs of any Gulf state, it must be recognized in advance by the United States that this is the role for which Iran is being primed and blame cannot be assigned for Iran's carrying out an implied assignment.[56]

The implementation of the Nixon Doctrine (followed and supported by President Carter) was in fact the continuation of more than a quarter century of U.S. imperialistic practices in the country. From the August, 1953 coup to the final days of the Pahlavi dynasty, the United States treated Iran as a client state. Furthermore, from the very beginning of its involvement in Iranian affairs the United States perceived the Iranian military as the principal instrument of its objectives in the country. (Until the inception of the Nixon Doctrine, however, U.S. military assistance to Iran consisted of loans and grants, which amounted to approximately $1.5 billion between 1946 and 1972. During this period more than 11,000 Iranian military personnel were trained in the United States.[57] Cold War rivalry and containment of domestic opposition to the monarchy were the twin motives behind United States military aid to Iran for these thirty years.)

Since the Pahlavi rule lacked any significant base of popular support, it was logical for the Shah to want constantly to expand the coercive base of his power, particularly in times of popular challenge to his rule. For example, in early 1960s, due to an intensified climate of disaffection, the National Front resumed its open activities and religious leaders became more vocal in their condemnation of the Pahlavi dictatorship. The Shah responded to this challenge by seeking to expand the military. In his book, *Kennedy*, Theodore Sorensen writes about the Shah's requests for arms in 1961,

> In Iran the Shah insisted on our supporting an expensive army too large for border incidents and internal security and of no use in an all out war. His army... resembled the proverbial man who was too heavy to do any light work and too light to do any heavy work.[58]

The Kennedy Administration refused the Shah's requests for more and better weapons. Instead, President Kennedy urged the Shah to begin social reforms in order to enlarge the middle class and pre-empted the opposition.

The Shah's "White Revolution" was definitely influenced by the pressure from the Kennedy Administration. However, realizing that his propaganda apparatus had already failed to project a reformist picture of his rule, he expanded the SAVAK and increased the repression of the opposition. The principal resistance to this intensified reign of terror came from the religious leaders. This resistance led to the mass rebellion of June 5, 1963, in which an estimated 15,000 Iranians were gunned down in the streets of Tehran, Shiraz, and Qom.[59] The leader of this rebellion was none other than Ayatollah Ruhollah Khomeini. The Iranian government immediately blamed "reactionary" mullahs for instigating the rebellion. The truth of the matter was that 1963 was the third consecutive year of an economic depression which had particularly hurt the lower classes in the cities—the elements of Iranian society most responsive to religious leadership.

The Shah's decision in the early 1970s to increase his military strength was once again influenced by the increased activities of the opposition, particularly the emergence of armed urban guerrillas.[60] However, the response of the Nixon Administration to the Shah's requests went far beyond the expectation of the Shah himself. It was the Nixon Doctrine which gave the Shah everything he asked for. The selling of conventional arms to a non-Western country without any restraint in regard to their quality, quantity and variety was a departure from the previous arms sale policies of the United States.

A surprising aspect of this dramatic change was that it had bipartisan support in Congress, and met with little criticism in the press or the academic community. The policy was justified, even as late as 1975, by the need to resist possible Soviet expansionism,

> The strategic, political, and economic importance of the Gulf countries to the U.S. and its Western allies is high and growing. Western Europe and Japan will remain dependent upon Gulf oil for years to come, and even our own dependence upon this oil is increasing, not diminishing. From a strategic point of view we have a clear interest in preventing the Soviet Union from exercising political, economic, or military hegemony over the area...[61]

U.S. officials at no time questioned the prudence of selling massive quantities of arms to a ruler whose regime relied upon severe internal repression for its continued existence. On the contrary, the U.S. viewed Iran as an island of stability in a troubled region. Since the Shah was clearly able to pay for whatever he requested, U.S. officials argued that it would be "politically difficult" to refuse him.[62] As late as July, 1977, when some questions concerning the logic of unrestrained arms sales to Iran were being raised in Congress, Senator Ribicoff expressed the sentiment of his colleagues when he said,

> Iran is one of the most important allies the United States has. When you realize that 50 percent of the world's oil comes through the Straits of Hormuz and the only armed forces to protect it are Iran's, to refuse him arms would be sheer stupidity on the part of the United States.[63]

From the beginning of the postwar period, Iran was viewed by U.S. policymakers as part of the global superpower conflict. The supposed threat of Soviet expansionism provided a convenient rationale for U.S. imperialist practices. The advent of detente did not effectively alter the basic components of U.S. policy toward Iran. While overt Soviet military aggression appeared a less distinct possibility, massive arms sales to Iran were justified by the U.S. need to pre-empt any Soviet attempt to control the flow of Iranian oil. In the view of U.S. officials, since the Western allies could not survive a shutoff of the oil spigot, the Shah of Iran had to become America's policeman in the Persian Gulf.

Cold war rivalry provided a backdrop for the development of a U.S.-Iranian relationship based upon imperialist domination by the former. This state of affairs was advantageous for the U.S. ruling elite as well as for the Shah. U.S. emphasis on maintaining the reactionary status quo coincided with the Shah's need for U.S. aid to bolster the coercive basis of his regime. Consequently, 30 years of U.S. policy toward Iran linked survival of the Shah's regime with the officially perceived U.S. national interest.

Given this framework, it is not surprising that U.S. officials were taken aback by the Iranian revolution. Washington badly underestimated the scope of Iranian opposition to the Shah because the logic of U.S. policies lacked any concern for the needs, dignity and the severe repression of the Iranian people. Indeed, U.S. officials remarked in retrospect that unofficial State Department policy precluded even contacts with the Iranian opposition leaders.[64]

The success of the Iranian revolution exposed the misconception behind U.S. policies toward Iran, particularly the Nixon Doctrine. The Shah's public relations apparatus nurtured a number of myths about Iran. Until very recently, these deceptive efforts were amplified by official Washington, which had long since come to believe the myths it had helped create about Iran.

In the selling of the Shah, the central myth that stitched all the others together was echoed in the now famous 1978 New Year's Eve toast delivered by President Carter at the Niavaran Palace in Tehran. Raising his glass under the glittering chandeliers, Carter proclaimed,

> Iran under the great leadership of the Shah is an island of stability in one of the most troubled areas of the world. This is a great tribute to you, your Majesty, and to your leadership and to the respect, admiration, and love which your people give to you.[65]

The myth of Iran's stability was predominant in the minds of U.S. policymakers for years. The president's toast to the Shah could have been uttered by any one of five other presidents, beginning with Dwight Eisenhower.

How did the myth of stability take hold? Exactly what was it that the CIA or the State Department failed to bring to Washington's attention?

One answer lies in the idea of political stability itself, an idea badly misunderstood in Washington. Stability defined in real, rather than abstract, terms requires an economic and political environment in which a population perceives its life as more or less satisfactory, or at least has hope of its becoming so. Most definitions also take account of the need for minimal tacit consent to a government's values and priorities. Neither of these criteria fit Iran under the Shah's rule. More than a half-million

Iranians were imprisoned for political reasons during the 25 years after the Shah was restored to power in the 1953 coup.

Another problem was that official Washington badly underestimated the character of the Iranian people, their ability and will to resist. Even after the fact, CIA director Stansfield Turner still could not understand what had happened,

> It was like a series of volcanoes bubbling up. But it certainly appeared that no one of them would bubble up so much that the government couldn't control it. What we didn't forecast was that...a 78-year-old cleric who had been in exile for 14 years would be the catalyst... and that we would have one huge volcano—a truly national revolution.[66]

Indeed, they did not forecast it. A CIA report released in the summer of 1978 indicates why Turner was so surprised, "Iran is not a revolutionary or even pre-revolutionary situation," the report reassured the Carter administration. "Those who are in opposition, both violent and nonviolent, do not have the capacity to be more than troublesome."[67]

In brief, then, U.S. foreign policy makers had come to confuse the notion of political stability with the Shah's ability to keep the lid on. This problem of equating coercion with consent was compounded by a view of Iranians as another Third World people simply too incompetent to shape their own destiny.

The popular revolution in Iran should not have come as such a surprise to the U.S. leaders. The realities of Iran under the Shah were not concealed. Even a quick reading of Iranian history would show that the people have an old and rich tradition of resisting tyranny; that all of Iran's popular political heroes were killed or imprisoned by ruling monarchs; that the confrontation between the absolute monarchy and liberalizing forces had been going on for a hundred years; that the monarchy was defeated in 1911 and 1951—only to be restored by a Western power (England in 1921 and the United States in 1953); that between 1953 and 1977 many thousands of the Shah's opponents were gunned down by the army—about two thousand of them officially executed; and that during this period more than half a million Iranians served time in prison for their opposition to the regime. It might have been deduced from these facts that the Iranians were not going to be indifferent to Henry Kissinger's designs on their lives and resources.

Thus, the U.S. government did not lack accurate information about Iran. Rather, its leaders lacked an understanding of a people who had long been exploited and oppressed by their rulers, and the leaders assumed that Iran was nothing more than the Shah, that his satisfaction was all that mattered in the relations between the two nations. U.S. leaders also assumed that the Iranian people lacked the capacity for authentic rebellion, and thus their collective actions against the Shah must have been instigated by a conspiracy. Conspiracies can be stopped if they are detected in time. Thus, what the government officials and the media actually mean by "failure of intelligence" could best be described as failure to uncover the conspiracies that fueled the revolution.

Kissenger once remarked in an interview with James Reston of the *New York Times* that "we (the U.S.A) really lack a philosophy for how to shape a new political evolution."[68] Richard Falk describes this remark as a "striking admission of the emptiness of cold war liberalism. What Kissinger did not recognize was that, given an imperialist foreign policy, the long-lasting 'satisfaction' with the status quo is not an aberration—a mere 'trouble,' as Kissinger put it—but an objective, structural requirement."[69]

The need to develop a philosophy which can guide the United States of America to shape "a new political evolution" is indeed a challenging opportunity for a society that rightfully prides itself for its innovative capabilities. But the response to the challenge, alas, may well be Kissingerian realism, for imperialism as a "structural requirement" of corporate capitalism militates against a more creative response. And yet, those who cannot be satisfied by Kissingerian realism must analyze the nature of the challenge and struggle for a humane alternative.

Footnotes: Chapter 6

1. James A. Field, Jr., *The Annals of the American Academy of Political and Social Sciences* (May 1972), p. 2.
2. John S. Badeau, *The American Approach to the Arab World* (New York: Harper & Row, 1963), pp. 15-33.
3. Field, *Political and Social Sciences*, p. 6.
4. Ibid., p. 5
5. Harry Magdoff, *The Age of Imperialism* (New York: Monthly Review Press, 1969), p. 174.
6. Field, *Political and Social Sciences*, p. 6.
7. Ibid., p. 19.
8. Ibid., p. 20.
9. Ibid., p. 13.
10. John DeNano, "The Movement for an Aggressive American Oil Policy Abroad," *American Historical Review* (July 1956), p. 858.
11. Raymond A. Hare, "The Great Divide: World War II," *The Annals of the American Academy of Political and Social Sciences* (May 1972), p. 28.
12. Joe Stork, *Middle East Oil and the Energy Crisis* (New York: Monthly Review Press, 1975), p. 23.
13. Ibid., p. 26.
14. Ibid., p. 350.
15. Ibid., p. 324-333.
16. Hare, "The Great Divide," p. 28.
17. Stork, *Middle East Oil*, p. 36.
18. Richard W. Cottam, *Nationalism in Iran* (Pittsburgh: University of Pittsburgh Press, 1964), pp. 216-217.
19. Harvey O'Connor, *World Crisis in Oil* (New York: Monthly Review Press 1962).
20. Richard Allen, *Imperialism and Nationalism in the Fertile Crescent* (New York: Oxford University Press, 1975), pp. 436-437.
21. Richard Barnet, *The Roots of War* (Baltimore: Penguin Books, 1972), p. 322.
22. Ibid.
23. Norman A. Graebner, *Cold War Diplomacy, 1945-1960* (New York: D. Van Nostrand, 1962), p. 171.
24. Ibid., pp. 171-176.
25. Ibid.
26. "The Middle East," *Congressional Quarterly* (Washington, D.C.: Congressional Quarterly, Inc., Third Edition, 1977), pp. 82-83.
27. Robert Curry, "USAID's Development Assistance Function,"

(Unpublished: California State Univ. at Sacramento, Economics Dept.)

28. James A. Bill and Carl Leiden, *Politics: Middle East* (Boston: Little, Brown and Company, 1979), pp. 217-236.

29. Eqbal Ahmad, "A World Restored Revisited: American Diplomacy in the Middle East," *Race and Class*, vol. XVIII, no. 3 (Winter 1976), pp. 248-249.

30. Don Peretz, *The Middle East Today* (New York: Holt, Rinehart, and Winston, 1978), pp. 251-254.

31. "The Middle East," *Congressional Quarterly*, pp. 82-83.

32. Ibid., pp. 55-56.

33. Eqbal Ahmad, "A World Revisited,", p. 241.

34. *The Sacramento Bee*, 30 July 1979, p. 1.

35. Edmond R. Hannauer, "Israeli Settlements," *Inquiry* (30 October 1978), pp. 13-15.

36. "The Middle East," *Congressional Quarterly*, pp. 109-113.

37. Janice J. Terry, *Attitudes of United States Congressmen Toward Aid to the Palestinians and Arms to Israel* (Beirut: Palestine Research Center, 1973).

38. Noam Chomsky, *Peace in the Middle East?* (New York: Penguin Books, 1976), pp. 53-54.

39. Ibid.

40. Terry, *Attitudes*, pp. 5-11.

41. "U.S. Policy Toward Iran Hearings" House of Representatives, Subcommittee on Europe and the Middle East (Washington, D.C.: January 1979), pp. 1-2.

42. "Mutual Defense Assistance Program, 1950," Hearings, Senate Foreign Relations Committee (Washington, D.C., June 1950), p. 79.

43. "Access To Oil—The U.S. Relationships With Saudi Arabia And Iran,"Staff Report Senate Committee on Energy and Mutual Resources (Washington, D.C.: December 1977), p. 101.

44. Ibid., p. 73.

45. "New Perspectives on the Persian Gulf," Hearings, Subcommittee on the Near East and South Asia (Washington, D.C.: June-July 1973), p. 95.

46. "The Persian Gulf, 1975: The Continuing Debate On Arms Sales," Hearings, Special Subcommittee On Investigations (Washington, D.C. , June 1975), pp. 80-81.

47. Richard Nixon, *U.S. Foreign Policy for the 1970s: Building for Peace* (Washington, D.C.: Government Printing Office, 1971), p. 20.

48. Ibid., p. 33.

49. Michael T. Klare, *War Without End* (New York: Vintage Books, 1972); also, Raphael Littauer and Norman Uphoff, *The Air War In Indochina* (Boston: Beacon Press, 1972).

50. Anthony Sampson, *The Arms Bazaar* (New York: Viking Press, 1977), p. 243.

51. R.M. Burrell, *The Persian Gulf* (New York: Library Press, 1972), pp. 9-12.

52. Sampson, *The Arms Bazaar*, p. 252.

53. William A. Dorman and Mansour Farhang, "Nobody Lost Iran," *Politics Today* (May-June 1979), pp. 32-37.

54. Ibid.

55. Richard Falk, "Iran and American Geopolitics in the Gulf," *Race and Class* (Summer 1979), pp. 46-47.

56. "Access To Oil" Senate Committee on Energy, p. 84.

57. "Middle East Oil," *Congressional Quarterly*, p. 82.

58. Theodore Sorensen, *Kennedy* (New York: Harper & Row, 1965), p. 628.

59. Richard Cottam, *Nationalism In Iran* (Pittsburgh: University of Pittsburgh Press, 1964), p. 308.

60. Fred Halliday, *Arabia Without Sultans* (New York: Vintage Books, 1974), p. 16.

61. "The Persian Gulf, 1975," Subcommittee on Investigations, p. 81.

62. Ibid., p. 177.

63. "Middle East Oil," *Congressional Quarterly*, p. 16.

64. "The U.S. Policy Toward Iran," Subcommittee on the Middle East, pp. 57-59.

65. Dorman and Farhang, "Nobody Lost Iran," p. 32.

66. Ibid., p. 33.

67. Ibid.

68. Falk, "Iran and American Geopolitics," p. 47.

69. Ibid.

CHAPTER 7

THE FUTURE OF IMPERIALISM AND THE STRUGGLE FOR A HUMANE WORLD

There are two primary questions involved in the study of imperialism as a transnational system of privilege: 1) the empirical question of whether or not such a system in fact exists; and 2) the theoretical question of what conditions and perceptions have led to its development.

The secondary questions of theoretical and empirical nature arise from the fact that the system of transnational privilege is not and cannot be monolithic. It is plagued by contradictions from within and challenged by forces from without. From within, the growing competition between Japan, the United States and Europe in the markets of the world is disrupting the dominant position of the United States. The present U.S. trade deficit is one manifestation of this development. If this trend continues it could lead to disruption in certain sectors of the U.S. economy and growth of unemployment among the industrial workers.

So far the world-wide competition among industrial capitalist countries has remained in the economic and financial realm, but sooner or later it will involve political and security issues as well. The Trilateral Commission symbolizes the desire of the competitors to deal with the situation within the boundaries of their common privileged position.[1]

Another internal source of tension for the dominant countries in the transnational system is the moral opposition from a cross-class segment of their populations. This moral opposition is numerically small and as yet politically insignificant, but it plays a vital role in exposing the deceptive character of the system and analyzing its destructive consequences for peace and justice.

The moral opposition (not the entire opposition) to the war in Vietnam within the United States can be viewed as the most political manifestation of the moral opposition to the structure of transnational privilege. It was the second time in the history of imperialism that a significant number of the citizens in the imperialist country engaged in an intense and sustained struggle against their own government's actions in a foreign nation. The first example of such opposition to an imperialist war took place in France during the French-Algerian War, although French opposition to the Algerian War was much less intense than U.S. opposition to the Vietnam War. The current discussion of human rights as an aspect of foreign policy within the U.S. government is in part a response to the pressure from the moral opposition. The most profound achievement of the moral opposition to United States imperialism is the level of public awareness which has made it extremely difficult for Washington to take overt or covert military action in defense of dominant elites in the subordinated societies.

A third source of tension within the transnational system lies in the frequent tactical disagreements between the privileged elites in the subordinated societies and the United States foreign policy makers. Facing the revolutionary challenge to the structure of privilege at home is not the same thing as fearing such a challenge from Washington. Managing a political system based on fear and coercion is quite a different role than running an empire from within an open society with a democratic tradition.

The deposed Shah of Iran could never understand why Richard Nixon had to resign the presidency of the United States. The dominant elites in countries such as Brazil, Chile, the Philippines, Indonesia and South Africa, among others, are often frustrated with the "slowness" and "cautiousness" of U.S. foreign policy making. They often complain about the inability of United States decision makers to "understand" their situation and make "binding commitments" to defend them. After United States bombers and troops killed more than a million Vietnamese and defoliated thousands of acres of forest, the Saigon elites were still complaining about the "cautiousness" and "indecisiveness" of the U.S. in conducting the war. The deposed Shah purchased more than twenty billion dollars worth of sophisticated weapons and military technology from the United States in ten years and he was still complaining about the United States' inability to respond with greater speed to his arms requests. Of course there is a contradiction between democracy and imperialism, but so far this contradiction has been dealt with at the expense of democracy.

Another source of tension related to the United States' "democratic indecisiveness" is the conflict between U.S. imperialist strategy and regional rivalries. The Middle East is a clear example of such conflict. The historic rivalry between Iran and Saudi Arabia was exploited and intensified in the 1970s by the U.S. arms sales to Iran. The Israeli military might, for the most part a U.S. gift to the Jewish State, frightens the U.S. Arab allies; and arms sales to Saudi Arabia and Egypt irritate Israel. There is a deadly logic to the United States' strategy in the region, but the strategy does not always coincide with the U.S. allies' perceptions of their own interests.

Besides the actual or potential revolutionary threat to the structure of power within the subordinated societies, there are three other sources of challenge to the transnational system of privilege. First, Soviet social imperialism is challenging the system of western privilege wherever the opportunity presents itself. Given Soviet imperialism in Eastern Europe and the repressiveness of its domestic rule, it can be argued that the Russian policymakers are not challenging the existing system of privilege in the interest of justice or freedom. However, absence of honorable intentions on the part of the Soviet leaders should not be confused with the fact that in many countries throughout the world the Soviet Union has aided the progressive and liberation movements against the forces of reaction. Cuba, Chile, Vietnam, Angola and Mozambique are the outstanding examples. This is not to claim that the Soviet Union has no design for using these revolutionary regimes for its own imperialist aims. The important point is that when Soviet policies toward the underdeveloped countries are judged by their consequences, they constitute a source of challenge to the existing system of privilege in the world.

The second outside source of challenge to the system of transnational privilege lies in the example and ideological pronouncements of the established revolutionary regimes such as China, Vietnam, Cuba and Iran. These countries inspire the revolutionary struggles throughout the world. Cuba is the only one which has militarily participated in a number of anti-western armed struggles in Africa. In its propaganda literature China often appears as a compassionate opponent of the structure of privilege in the world. But given its present tendency to oppose whatever the Soviet Union is for, China seems hesitant to give even moral support to those liberation movements which have the potential to be exploited by the Soviet Union.

The third outside source of challenge to the system of transnational privilege is located in the progressive nationalist regimes seeking a more equitable definition of the international economic order. Nations like Algeria, India, Yugoslavia and China can be placed in this category. The multinational corporations do not have a free hand in these countries, for the satisfaction of basic human needs has been given priority over the development of the market for consumer goods.

During the Cold War "national security" was the favorite slogan of the United States foreign policy makers. The requirements of national security were supposed to explain and justify subversion, militarism and war. The national security arguments were greatly enhanced by the scholarly or academic analyses of international politics, which viewed the threat to national security as a permanent and universal feature of politics among nations. The rhetoric of national security and the so-called realist analyses of international politics epitomized a particular way of reacting to the events in the world.

The issues that appeared to concern the national security managers during the Cold War era were mostly related to the alleged Soviet military aggressiveness, as well as revolution and radicalization of nationalism in the Third World. During this period the seeming absence of international economic concerns from the rhetoric of policymakers and scholars was due to the fact that the United States was already dominating world commerce.

Now the rhetoric of national security is often replaced by the rhetoric of interdependence. Former Secretary of State Henry Kissinger officially began the new rhetoric in his address before the Sixth Special Session of the United Nations General Assembly. "We are all engaged in a common enterprise. No nation or group of nations can gain by pushing beyond the limits that sustain world economic growth. No one benefits from basing progress on tests of strength."[2]

There is some truth to the rhetoric of interdependence insofar as it relates to the interests of the advanced industrial states. The issues involved in this interdependence are unrelated to the topic of this essay simply because they do not involve imperialist relationships. The industrial capitalist states are competing partners within their common privileged position. When there is a congruence of interests between two advanced industrial states, it can lead to reciprocal gains by the societies concerned. But the principle of reciprocal gains for the society at large seldom applies to those underdeveloped countries in which the rigid class structure and absence of consensus politics make the interests of the state, which represents the privileged few, antagonistic to the interests of the populace.

The new significance of interdependence with respect to the subordinated countries in the transnational system of privilege is in some ways akin to the national security symbolism of the Cold War era; interdependence is intended to serve the interests of the United States and justify the defense of the status quo in the class-ridden underdeveloped nations.

It is certain that imperialism as a transnational system of privilege has produced an unprecedented amount of resentment among the populace in the subordinated societies. This resentment, which is a response to exploitation, coercion and consumption-oriented manipulation, has resulted in an intensified and expanded revolutionary challenge from below. Thus, installation of repression technology in the dominated society and militarization of its state have become necessary in order to maintain the status quo. And yet it is a mistake to think of the export of manipulation, repression and militarism to the underdeveloped countries as a reaction to the resentment of the wretched. Since the resentment itself is a product of imperialism, the response to it is also a product of imperialism. Seen in this light, repression and militarism are the organic commodities of imperialism in search of global markets. No wonder, therefore, that our world is plagued with misery, repression and violence.

It is sad to say that too many of the Third World governments are anxious customers for the latest commodities of imperialism. Too many of them spend the precious resources of their peoples in a parasitic and paranoia-producing arms race. Too many of them are more responsive to the greed of the few for luxury goods than to the essential needs of the many. The arms race and the insatiable hunger for luxury goods are integral parts of the imperialist design for the contemporary world. Too many Third World leaders are the unconscious victims of imperialism. The perceptions which were imposed on their fathers by colonialism and imperialism have gradually become so internalized that they consider them to be the product of their own thinking. Cultural imperialism has penetrated the deepest levels of their psyches. It is indeed painful to admit that too many Third World governments use the imported instruments of repression and oppression against their own peoples more indiscriminately than their producers intend.

Why did China have to teach Vietnam a lesson? What justification was there for the Pol Pot regime in Cambodia to pursue a course of action that resulted in the needless deaths of many of its own citizens? If the new regime in Cambodia is popular and legitimate, why are foreign troops compelled to continue their presence in the country? The rebellion in Afghanistan has produced tens of thousands of deaths and refugees as a result of the military operations by Russian troops in the country. The irrational and alienated national leaders justify such actions in the name of an imported "ism." It does not matter that the natives reject the imported formula or do not wish to be represented by those who arrogate scientific mission to themselves.

The progressive elements in the Third World and their allies in the imperialist societies betray their own lack of commitment to economic welfare, human rights and peace when they respond to issues such as the ones raised above in an evasive and superficial manner. It was not class struggle or economic considerations which produced the latest tragedies in Indochina. And it is not enough to claim that subjective factors are at work without pursuing the question of exactly what we mean by subjective factors, where they originate, how they evolve and what should be done about them. It must be recognized that a Marxist or other materialist theories of conflict fall short of explaining the problems of our time. There is more than enough historical evidence to prove that materialist explanations and prescriptions, whether rooted in Marxism or capitalism, neither fully comprehend the nature of human conflicts nor sufficiently satisfy human aspirations.

The revolutionary experiences of this century are once again demonstrating the ancient truth that the struggle for justice, freedom, peace and independence requires a moral dimension which is separate from and beyond the material structure. Nuclear weapons and the real possibility of their use have intensified, in an unprecedented manner, the need for this recognition. The 19th century conditions of growth and industrialization made morality subservient to materialism in social theories and political actions. The contemporary revolutionary movements can no longer continue on this path if they intend to produce a more humane socio-political environment.

What is needed in the contemporary world is a moral and global anti-imperialist struggle. Much has been said about the roots or causes of misery, repression and violence. The important point about all such analyses in our time is that the survival of the international community itself has come to depend on collective efforts to produce a more humane world. Since the structure of misery, repression and violence in the contemporary world is transnational, any moral opposition to this structure must also be transnational. This does not mean that the struggle against imperialism should negate national identity. Rather it is a new definition of national identity which is needed in a transnational movement toward economic welfare, human rights and peace.

The philosophy of power born by the requirements of imperialist expansion has become the ideology of the dominant faction of the foreign policy elites in the U.S. For these elements, any thought that does not conform to the generation and accumulation of power as the guiding principle of foreign policy making is a nuisance. "Instant moralists," "isolationists," "naive idealists" are some of the more popular terms the foreign policy elites use to describe those who object to the unlimited pursuit of power in world politics. The formulators and administrators of United States imperialist policies have adopted a code of manners which benefits the type of policymaker to whom the most unacceptable behavior is to lose one's coolness.

During the 1950s, preoccupation with perceived Soviet military aggressiveness and context-free memories of history provided an emotional situation in which even many of the humanistic intellectuals failed to see the reality of U.S. imperialism. The United States was in a mood of tribal nationalism and its people, like all tribal nationalists, were too preoccupied with the Enemy to see the essential brutality of their foreign policies toward the Third World.

U.S. imperialism is committed to, as its permanent objective, the protection of the transnational system of privilege. It is interested neither in the assimilation of the client states nor in their temporary exploitation. Such a notion in international politics was not even in existence before the rise of imperialism in the 19th century. The United States has inherited this perspective from its European predecessors. However, the idea of expansion as an end in itself is not political in its origin. As Hannah Arendt writes of 19th century imperialism,

> Expansion as a permanent and supreme aim of politics is the central political idea of imperialism. Since it implies neither temporary looting nor the more lasting assimilation of conquest, it is an entirely new concept in the long history of political thought and action. The reason for this surprising originality—surprising because entirely new concepts are very rare in politics—is simply that this concept is not really political at all, but has its origin in the realm of business speculation, where expansion meant the permanent broadening of industrial production and economic transaction characteristic of the nineteenth century.[3]

The possibility of economic growth, that is, expansion and efficiency in the process of production, is "as unlimited as the capacity of man to produce for, establish, furnish, and improve on the human world."[4]

The well-established nation-state system does not allow the United States to claim openly that it is imposing a superior law upon barbarians. Those days seem to have ended. The contemporary imperialist creed must be acceptable to both the citizens of the mother country and the administrators of the imperialist network. Thus, faithfulness to the prerogatives of self-determination is indispensable if imperialism is going to receive the necessary popular support on the home front. It is therefore no wonder that the policymakers have often been secretive or deceptive in explaining their actions to the public. The "secret bombing" of Cambodia in 1969 could not have been secret from the Cambodians. It is only through the creation and perpetuation of false consciousness in its own citizens that a popularly elected government can engage in secret bombing of another country.

Thus, an anti-imperialist view of society has to be based on a rational determination of human interests. Interests are generalized means which increase the ability of human beings to get what they want. From a radical perspective interests are defined as long-run, rational and always committed to the common good of the society.[5] Members of one economic class do not necessarily, potentially or actually have a common subjective view of their own situation. Subjective common interests must involve a moral dimension which transcends the immediate material conditions. Imperialism cannot be defeated in a confrontation that is limited to material motives. Only a struggle with a moral dimension which is separate from and beyond material concerns can offer an alternative to imperialism.

For serious and committed students of human affairs, negation of the given and rejection of false and hypocritical solutions to the problems of injustice, violence and alienation are the prerequisites for any positive analysis or formulation of viable alternatives. The emphasis on negation is crucial because, as Marcuse writes,

> the truly positive is the society of the future and therefore beyond definition and determination, while the existing positive is that which must be surmounted. But the experience and understanding of the existent society may well be capable of identifying what is not conducive to free and rational society, what impedes and distorts the possibilities of its creation.[6]

In other words, formulation of concrete and constructive alternatives to capitalist imperialism would greatly weaken the prevailing modes of thought and behavior. Thus, a negative but rational and humane analysis of the society constitutes the foundation of any positive effort concerning what is to be done. The validity of negation,[7] therefore, does not depend on the immediate availability of practical alternatives; it can only be challenged on its own grounds, which include a radical and moral view of people and society.

The imperialist powers do not have to give anything in order to change the transnational system of privilege; they should simply stop robbing and interfering. Given the finiteness of natural resources, it is destructive for six percent of the world's population to consume more than thirty percent of the world's oil. For besides the obvious economic unfairness in such distribution, the consequent inequities are easily translated into coercive power that is used to intervene militarily. As Galtung has written,

> Moves toward more proportionate consumption will have to be taken. At this point it is important to note that this reasoning is increasingly accepted when the Center overconsumes resources taken from the Periphery. Tomorrow we may, however, go one step further in our thinking and define certain resources as belonging to humankind as a whole, no matter where they are located.

A transnational movement against imperialism must make a distinction between military self-defense and intervention in the dominated societies; it must expose the inequitable and exploitative practices of the transnational corporations and develop mechanisms to make them more accountable; and it must engage in political mobilization for structural change rather than in charitable activities. This is not to say that the transfer of capital and knowledge from the industrial to the dependent societies is not desirable. What we need is a new concept of technical assistance. Galtung has made a significant contribution to the development of this concept by dealing with the questions of "what is the best setting for technical assistance, what should be the content, and how can one diminish the asymmetry between donors and recipients?"[8]

A transnational movement against imperialism must be inclusive, not exclusive. Dogmatic theories of history, linear or nonlinear, often become tools in the hands of oppressors. New social forms come into being through human choice and will. In this struggle, the liberal emphasis on values, the religious emphasis on morality and the Marxist emphasis on contradictions have to be combined in both analysis and action. The actors come from the exploited peoples of the Third World and from the circles of their moral supporters. In this sense the Third World is not a geographic designation; it is a structural concept as well as a designation for the exploited peoples everywhere.

> In general, structural reasoning leads to more complex maps of social reality than classroom maps are able to reflect. Moreover, contradictions...are multiple, even unlimited in number, and will always be with us. But in each concrete case—with specific answers to the questions of *where* and *when*—there is usually one contradiction that is more important than the others and should be attacked *first*. However, and significantly, in deciding which contradiction is most important I would look at *how much* it impedes the satisfaction of *how basic* needs for *how many*; not at some theory about possible linkages between one contradiction and others.[8]

Galtung has developed the idea of *self-reliance* into a conceptual guide for collective and individual action in the struggle against inequity, exploitation and dependence. His prescriptions are detailed, creative and comprehensive. The readers of this book are strongly urged to study Galtung's *The True Worlds: A Transnational Perspective* and pay special attention to his theory of progressive action, particularly his challenging analysis of self-reliance as the overriding strategy for structural changes in local, national, international and transnational settings.

Galtung believes that both the capitalist and the socialist types of imperialism are in various conflicts and contradictions. They both use means of coercion to perpetuate their repressive and exploitative structures. "Thus the world gets a war system, in addition to the dominance system, in the form of East-West arms race, and in the form of imperialistic wars." The strategy of self-reliance must include holding onto raw materials and importing fewer industrial goods for those under the domination of capitalistic imperialism and organized resistance or disobedience for those suffering under social imperialism.

> In both cases one may have to wait until the suppressing country or countries are weak, preparing for the moment to come.... Weakness may come about by

> withholding from them what they like most, a demand for economic products or a corresponding demand for ideological products. Ultimately the weakness may also be brought about through the finiteness of nature.[9]

The existence of politics connotes that there is more than one choice in establishing social priorities and managing public affairs. These choices are not equally just or pleasant, but simply possible. In the absence of an effective choice there can be no political action, for action implies intention and intentionality means choosing one mode of perception over another. Thus, logically, U.S. imperialism is the product of choices made by human beings and thus it can be changed or modified by decisions made by human beings. Since war is no longer a rational or likely means of ending imperialist policies, only a qualitative change in the values and priorities of imperialist societies can end imperialism.

The critique of capitalist imperialism presented in this book is derived from a humanistic conception of social change which assumes the existence of politics under all circumstances. This conception perceives economic development as basically a qualitative phenomenon. According to this view, growth in the material conditions of existence should serve to end oppression, minimize suffering and maximize freedom. The value of quantitative progress depends on its capacity to achieve these objectives. In other words, material growth should serve humanity, not the other way around.

Soviet-type socialism has yet to answer the question of how human aspirations are expected to develop after the satisfaction of fundamental needs. It is due to the refusal of the Soviet Union to accept socio-political freedom as a moral/psychological need that social imperialism has produced one of the most repressive systems in world history. So long as such recognition is missing in the actual operation of the Soviet system, the practice of repression will inevitably expand and intensify.

Historically, quantitative achievements have constituted the preconditions for the expansion of human freedom. This experiential lesson seems to be universally true because satisfaction of basic human needs has always been a prerequisite for any qualitative change in the human condition. Such qualitative change, however, does not follow automatically. Material growth can lead to a less exploitative existence only through people's conscious efforts and a systematic restructuring of the competitive and scarcity-oriented modes of thought and behavior, that is to say, the kind of consciousness and expectations which can be subjected to unending manipulation for profit-making. It is this perverted mode of consciousness which is blocking a potential challenge to imperialism within the U.S. society.

So long as the economic system has to create feelings of deprivation for its existence and growth, the society as a whole will remain supportive of or indifferent to imperialism as a functional system of privilege. It is unlikely that any substantive portion of the society can become concerned with moral issues, particularly in regard to international relations, when the socio-economic structure encourages the individual to be preoccupied with the self to the point of alienating one from oneself and from one's community. Thus, while technological advancement has made qualitative social change a possibility for the first time, the dominant culture continues to socialize its children with the pre-technological notions of competition and growth. Schumpeter's concept of imperialism as atavism—"the dead always rule the living"—is more relevant today than at the time he wrote his analysis of imperialism.

Modern technology has the potential to end imperialism and free people from the bonds of toil and repression by abolishing the condition of material need as an effective stimulus for human behavior. To do this, the overriding principle of the political organization of technology must be the maximization of freedom from necessity. There is a profound incompatibility between such a rationally constituted social system and the imperialist order. In the rational system, using the words of the noted economist Robert Heilbroner,

> the world of science, as it is applied by society, is committed to the idea of man as a being who shapes his collective destiny; the world of capitalism to an

> idea of man as one who permits his common social destination to take care of itself. The essential idea of a society built on scientific engineering is to impose human will on the social universe; that of capitalism to allow the social universe to unfold as if it were beyond human interference.[10]

A rationally constituted system is based on reason and equity; imperialism demands blind obedience and subordination. Science and technology guided by reason can become vehicles of liberation, while their blind application for accumulation of wealth and power can only lead to domination and repression. Of course there is nothing new about repression; it has always been a central fact of the human condition. Wherever people exploit each other, wherever they are treated as means rather than ends, repression, which is the conscious or unconscious submission to toil and self-denial, is the outcome. Historically repression has been the result of two interrelated conditions. First, the existence of scarcity, which was largely an inescapable fact of nature. Second, the general acceptance of cultural taboos and restrictions as the guiding principles of human interaction. Science and historical experience show that both of these conditions are sociologically determined and have little, if anything, to do with human nature.

Human liberation is obtainable only after the permanent unchaining of human beings from mere necessity, namely, abolition of the first cause of repression. Once this objective is achieved, the second cause of repression can be expected to decrease and deteriorate. It is not too difficult to prove that cultural taboos and restrictions have always provided the psychological forces of law and order in perpetuating the status quo. U.S. society has reached a stage of material growth in which the permanent unchaining of men and women from mere necessity can be realized. But capitalist imperialism and its concomitant ideology resist the realization of this old dream simply because such a development is detrimental to the continuation of deprivation-oriented consciousness, which is a prerequisite for growth as an end in itself.

Just as corporate capitalism perpetuates deprivation and anxiety in the interest of growth, the practice of imperialism aggravates misery and violence in the name of security. The common philosophical denominator of corporate capitalism and imperialism is the cult of every person for himself or herself, which is a principal source of alienation and existential misery as well as prime cause of inequity, exploitation and dependence.

Footnotes: Chapter 7

1. Robert O. Koehane and Joseph S. Nye, *Power and Interdependence: World Politics in Transition* (Boston: Little, Brown and Co., 1977), p. 26.

2. Henry Kissinger, "A New National Partnership," *Department of State Bulletin*, 17 February 1975.

3. Hannah Arendt, *Imperialism* (New York: Harcourt, Brace and World, Inc., 1968). p. 5.

4. Ibid., p. 6.

5. "Common good" is used here to describe the interests of the community as a whole, as distinguished from "particular goods" pursued by rival groups. Common good is defined by rational means and its purpose is to move the society toward those conditions which enable the citizens to provide for their physical, intellectual, and moral needs. In striving to bring about such conditions, the state exercises protective and promotive functions.

6. Herbert Marcuse, *Repressive Tolerance* (Boston: Beacon Press, 1967), p. 87.

7. The concept of negation is used both logically and metaphysically. In its logical sense. negation is opposed to affirmation; it denies the validity or goodness of a situation or a proposition as contrasted with the act of affirming it. In its metaphysical sense, negation is the mere absence of a character or relation that is regarded as positive. Used logically the concept of negation is, by definition, committed to a system of values which is regarded as superior to the operational norms of the situation or character being negated. In the above context, negation is used in its logical sense and applies principally to values rather than structure.

8. Johan Galtung, *The True Worlds: A Transnational Perspective* (New York: Free Press, 1980), pp. 397 - 8.

9. Ibid., p. 423.

10. Robert Heilbroner and Arthur M. Ford, *Is Economics Relevant?* (Pacific Palisades, Goodyear Publishing Co., Inc., 1976), p. 285.

Bibliography

Abir, Mordechai. *Oil, Power and Politics*. London: Frank Cass, 1974.

———. *The Persian Gulf as a Focus for Regional Conflicts*. New York: Transaction Books, 1977.

Abrams, Richard M., Ed. *The Issues of the Populist and Progressive Eras, 1892-1912*. New York: Harper & Row Pubs., Inc., 1971.

Abu-Lughod, Ibraihim, Ed. *The Transformation of Palestine*. Evanston, Ill.: Northwestern University Press, 1971.

Acheson, Dean. *Present at the Creation: My Years in the State Department*. New York: Norton, 1969.

———. *Power and Diplomacy*. Cambridge: Harvard University Press, 1958.

Adams, Michael and Christopher Mayhew. *Publish It Not...The Middle East Cover-Up*. New York: Longman, 1975.

Aguilar, Alonso. *Pan-Americanism, From Monroe to the Present*. New York: Monthly Review Press, 1968.

Alavi, Hamza. "Imperialism: Old and New," *Socialist Register 1964*. New York: Monthly Review Press, 1964.

Allen, Richard. *Imperialism and Nationalism in the Fertile Crescent*. New York: Oxford University Press, 1975.

Almond, Gabriel A. *The American People and Foreign Policy*. New York: Harcourt, Brace, Jovanovich, Inc., 1950.

Al-Marayati, Abid A. *The Middle East: Its Government and Politics*. Belmont, Calif.: Duxebury Press, 1972.

Alperovitz, Gar. *Atomic Diplomacy*. New York: Simon and Schuster, 1965.

AlRoy, Gil Carl. *Behind the Middle East Conflict: The Real Impasse Between Arab and Jew*. New York: Capricorn, 1975.

———. *The Kissinger Experience: American Policy in the Middle East*. New York: Horizon, 1975.

Amin, Samir. *Neo-Colonialism in West Africa*. New York: Monthly Review Press. 1974.

Anthony, John Duke. *Arab States of the Lower Gulf: People, Politics, Petroleum.* Washington: Middle East Institute, 1975.

Anthony, John Duke, Ed. *The Middle East: Oil, Politics, and Development*. Washington: American Enterprise Institute, 1975.

Aruri, Naseer H., Ed. *Middle East Crucible: Studies on the Arab-Israeli War of October 1973*. Wilmette, Ill.: Medina University Press, 1975.

Badeau, John S. *The American Approach to the Arab World.* New York: Harper & Row Pubs., Inc., 1963.

Baran, Paul and Paul M. Sweezy. *Monopoly Capital.* New York: Monthly Review Press, 1966.

Baran, Paul A. *The Political Economy of Growth*. New York: Monthly Review Press, 1975.

Barber, R. J. *The American Corporation: Its Power, Its Money, Its Politics.* New York: Dutton, 1970.

Barnet, Richard J. *The Crisis of the Corporation.* Washington, D.C.: Institute for Policy Studies, 1977.

———. *The Economy of Death.* New York: Atheneum, 1969.

———. *Intervention and Revolution.* New York: The World Publishing Co., 1968.

———. *The Roots of War.* Baltimore, Maryland: Penguin Books, 1972.

Barnet, Richard and Ronald Muller. *Global Reach.* New York: Simon and Schuster, 1974.

Beard, Charles and Mary. *A Basic History of the United States.* New York: Doubleday, Doran & Co.,1945.

Behrman, Jack. *Some Patterns in the Rise of the Multinational Enterprise.* New York: McGraw-Hill, 1969.

———. *U.S. International Business and Governments.* New York: McGraw-Hill, 1971.

Beisner, Robert L. *Twelve Against Empire: The Anti-Imperialist 1898-1900.* New York: McGraw-Hill, 1972.

Beloff, Max. *Foreign Policy and the Democratic Process.* Westport, Conn.: Greenwood Press, Inc., 1977.

Berding, Andrew H. *Dulles on Diplomacy.* New York: D. Van Nostrand, 1965.

Bergsten, C. Fred and Lawrence Krause, Eds. *World Politics and International Economics.* New York: Brookings Institute, 1975.

Bick, Barbara. *Culture and Politics.* Washington, D.C.: Institute for Policy Studies, 1976.

Bill, James A. *The Middle East: Politics and Power.* Boston: Allyn and Bacon, 1974.

Bill, James A. and Carl Leiden. *Politics: Middle East.* Boston: Little, Brown and Co., 1979.

Blair, John M. *The Control of Oil.*New York: Pantheon, 1976.

Bober, Arie. *The Other Israel: The Radical Case Against Zionism.* New York: Doubleday, 1972.

Bosch, Juan. *Pentagonism: A Substitute for Imperialism.* New York: Grove Press, 1968.

Brodine, Virginia and Mark Selden, Eds. *Open Secret: The Kissinger-Nixon Doctrine in Asia.* New York: Harper & Row Pubs., Inc., 1972.

Brown, Lester. *World Without Borders.* New York: Random House 1972.

Bullock, John. *The Making of a War: The Middle East from 1967 to 1973.* London: Longman, 1974.

Cameron, Kenneth N. *Humanity and Society: A World History.* New York: Monthly Review Press, 1977.

Carleton, William G. *The Revolution in American Foreign Policy: Its Global Range.* New York: Random House, 1967.

Carr, E.H. *Nationalism and After.* New York: MacMillan, 1945.

Chaliand, Gerard. *Revolution in the Third World.* New York: Penguin Books, 1978.

Chomsky, Noam. *Peace in the Middle East?* New York: Penguin Books, 1976.
Chomsky, Noam and Howard Zinn, Eds., *The Pentagon Papers: Critical Essays*. Boston: Beacon Press, 1972.
Chubin, Shahram. *The Foreign Relations of Iran: A Developing State in a Zone of Great-Power Conflict*. Berkeley: University of California Press, 1976.
Churba, Joseph. *The Politics of Defeat: America's Decline in The Middle East*. New York: Cyrco Press, 1977.
Clark, Grover. *The Balance Sheet of Imperialism*. New York: Columbia University Press, 1936.
Cline, Ray. *World Power Assessment*. Washington: Georgetown University Center for Strategic and International Studies, 1977.
Cohen, Aharon. *Israel and the Arab World*. Boston: Beacon, 1976.
Cohen, B.C.. *The Press and Foreign Policy*. New Jersey: Princeton University Press, 1963.
Cohen, Stephen D. and Red C. Bergsten. *The Making of United States International Economy Policy*. New York: Praeger Special Studies. 1978.
Congressional Quarterly. *The Middle East*. Washington, D.C.: Congressional Quarterly, Inc., Third Edition, 1977.
Cooper, Richard. *The Economics of Interdependence: Economic Policy in the Atlantic Community*. New York: McGraw-Hill, 1968.
Cottam, Richard. *Nationalism in Iran*. University of Pittsburgh Press, 1964.
Curtin, Philip D., Ed. *Imperialism*. New York: Harper Torchbooks, 1972.
Curtis, Michael, Ed. *People and Politics in the Middle East*. New York: Transaction Books, 1971.
De Beauvior, Simone. *The Mandarins*. Cleveland: Meridian, 1960.
De Novo, John A. *American Interests and Policies in the Middle East, 1900-1939*. Minneapolis: University of Minnesota Press, 1963.
De Riencourt, Amaury. *The American Empire*. New York: The Dell Publishing Co., 1968.
Deutscher, Isaac. *Revolutionary Essays*. Berkeley: The Ramparts Press, 1970.
Domhoff, G. William. *Who Rules America?* New Jersey: Englewood Cliffs, 1967.
Doran, Charles . *Myth, Oil and Politics*. New York: The Free Press, 1978.
Draper, John W. *Thoughts on the Future Civil Policy of America*. New York: Garland Publishers, 1867.
Draper, Theodore. *The Dominican Revolt: A Case Study in American Policy*. New York: Commentary, 1968.
Dulles, Foster R. *America's Rise to World Power: 1898-1954*. New York: Harper and Row Pubs., Inc., 1955.
Dulles, John F. *War or Peace*. New York: Macmillan, 1950.
Duroselle, Jean-Baptist. *From Wilson to Roosevelt: Foreign Policy of the United States, 1913-1945*. New York: Harper & Row Pubs., Inc., 1978.
Edwards, Richard, *et al.* Eds. *The Capitalist System: A Radical Analysis of American Society*.Englewood Cliffs, N.J.: Prentice-Hall, 1972.
El-Asmar, Rouzi. *To Be An Arab in Israel*. London: Frances Pinter. 1975.
Emmanuel, Arghiai. *Unequal Exchange: A Study of the Imperialism of Trade*. New York: Monthly Review Press, 1972.

Engler, Robert. *The Politics of Oil.* New York: Macmillan, 1961.
Fann, K.T. and Donald E. Hodges, Eds. *Readings in U.S. Imperialism.* Boston: Porter Sargent, 1971.
Fanon, Frantz. *The Wretched of the Earth.* New York: Grove Press, 1965.
Faulkner, Harold U. *American Economic History.* New York: Harper & Row Pubs., Inc., 1960.
———. *Politics, Reform and Expansion: 1890-1900.* New York: Harper & Row Pubs., Inc., 1960.
Finer, Herman. *Dulles Over Suez: The Theory and Practice of His Diplomacy.* Chicago: University of Chicago Press, 1964.
Finn, David. *The Corporate Oligarchy.* New York: Simon and Schuster, 1969.
Frank, A. G. *Latin America: Underdevelopment or Revolution.* New York: Monthly Review Press, 1970.
Freire, Paulo. *Pedagogy of the Oppressed.* New York: Seabury Press, 1970.
Galbraith, John K. *Economics and the Public Purpose.* Boston: Houghton-Mifflin, 1973.
Gilpin, Robert. *The Multinational Corporation and National Interest.* Washington,D.C.: Government Printing Office, 1973.
———. *U.S. Power and the Multinational Corporation.* New York: Basic Books, 1975.
Glassman, Jon D. *Arms for the Arabs: The Soviet Union and War in the Middle East.* Baltimore: John Hopkins University Press, 1976.
Golan, Matti. *The Secret Conversations of Henry Kissinger.* New York: Quadrangle, 1976.
Grant, James. *Multinational Corporations and the Developing Countries: The Emerging Job Crisis and Its Implications.* Washington, D.C.: Overseas Development Council, January, 1972.
Green, Mark, Ed. *Monopoly Makers.* New York: Grossman, 1973.
Greene, Felix. *The Enemy: What Every American Should Know About Imperialism.* New York: Vintage, 1971.
Gunter, Hans. *Transnational Industrial Relations.* London: Macmillan, 1973.
Haley, P.E. *Revolution and Intervention: The Diplomacy of Taft and Wilson with Mexico.* Boston, Mass.: M.I.T. Press, 1971.
Halliday, Fred. *Arabia Without Sultans.* New York: Vintage Books, 1974.
Harrison,, Selig S. *The Widening Gulf: Asian Nationalism and American Policy.* New York: The Free Press, 1978.
Hartmann, Frederick H. *The New Age of American Foreign Policy.* New York: Macmillan, 1970.
Hayes, C.J. *Essays on Nationalism.* New York: Harcourt, Brace, Jovanovich, 1926.
———. *The Historical Evolution of Modern Nationalism.* New York: Macmillan, 1948.
Hayter, Teresa. *Aid as Imperialism.* Middlesex: Pelican, 1971.
Heikal, Mohamed. *The Cairo Documents.* Garden City, New York: Doubleday, 1973.
Heilbroner, Robert L. *An Inquiry Into the Human Prospect.* New York: W.W. Norton & Company, 1974.

———. *The Great Ascent.* New York: Harper Torchbooks, 1963.
———. *The Limits of American Capitalism.* New York: Harper & Row Pubs., Inc., 1971.
Heilbroner, Robert and Arthur M. Ford. *Is Economics Relevant?* Pacific Palisades, Calif.: Goodyear Publishing Co., Inc., 1976.
Henry, Jules. *Culture Against Man.* New York: Random House, 1963.
Hobson, J.A. *Imperialism, A Study.* London: Allen and Unwin, 1948.
Hofstadter, Richard. *Social Darwinism in American Thought.* New York: George Braziller, Inc., 1959.
Horowitz, David, Ed. *Containment and Revolution.* Boston, Mass.: Beacon Press, 1962.
Horowitz, T.L. *Latin American Radicalism.* New York: Vintage Paperbacks, 1969.
Howe, Irving, Ed. *A Dissenter's Guide to Foreign Policy.* New York: Anchor, 1968.
Hurewitz, J.C. *The Arab-Israeli Dispute and the Industrial World.* Boulder, Colo.: Westview, 1976.
———. *Middle East Dilemmas: The Background of United States Policy.* New York: Russell and Russell, 1973.
———. *Middle East Politics: The Military Dimension.* New York: Octagon Books, 1974.
———. *The Struggle for Palestine.* New York: Shocken, 1976.
Hussain, Mehmood. *PLO.* Delhi, India: University Publishers, 1975.
Isaacs, Stephen D. *Jews and American Politics.* Garden City, New York: Doubleday, 1974.
Ismael, Tareq Y. *The Middle East in World Politics: A Study in International Relations.* Syracuse, New York: Syracuse University Press, 1974.
Jalee, Pierra. *Imperialism in the Seventies.* New York: Monthly Review Press, 1974.
———. *The Pillage of the Third World.* New York: Monthly Review Press, 1968.
Jiryis, Sabri. *The Arabs in Israel.* New York: Monthly Review Press, 1976.
Julien, Calude. *The American Empire.* Boston, Mass.: Beacon Press, 1971.
Jureidini, Paul A. and William E. Hazen. *The Palestinian Movement in Politics.* Lexington, Mass.: Lexington Books, 1976.
Kalecki, Michael, Ed. *Selected Essays on the Dynamics of the Capitalist Economy.* London: Cambridge University Press, 1971.
Katz, Samuel. *Battleground: Fact and Fantasy in Palestine.* New York: Bantam, 1973.
Kaufmann, William W. *The McNammara Strategy.* New York: Harper & Row Pubs., Inc., 1964.
Kennan, George. *American Diplomacy, 1900-1950.* Chicago: University of Chicago Press, 1952.
———. *Realities of American Foreign Policy.* Princeton: Princeton University Press, 1954.
Kindleberger, Charles. *Power and Money: The Economics of International Politics and the Politics of International Economics.* New York: Basic Books, 1970.

Kissinger, Henry A. *American Foreign Policy: Three Essays.* New York: Norton, 1969.

———. *Nuclear Weapons and Foreign Policy.* New York: Harper & Row Pubs., Inc., 1957.

Klare, Michael T. *Supplying Repression.* New York: The Field Foundation, 1977.

———. *War Without End.* New York: Vintage Books, 1972.

Koehane, Robert O. and Joseph S. Nye. *Power and Interdependence: World Politics in Transition.* Boston: Little, Brown, & Co., 1977.

———. *Transnational Relations and World Politics.* Boston: Harvard University Press, 1972.

Kohn, Hans. *The Idea of Nationalism.* New York: MacMillan, 1966.

Kolko, Gabriel. *The Politics of War.* New York: Vintage Books, 1968.

———. *The Roots of American Foreign Policy: An Analysis of Power and Purpose.* Boston: Beacon Press, Inc., 1969.

Kolko, Joyce and Gabriel Kolko. *The Limits of Power.* New York: Harper & Row Pubs., Inc., 1972.

Koury, Fred J. *The Arab-Israeli Dilemma.* New York: Knopf, 1976.

Kujawa, Duane, Ed. *American Labor and the Multinational Corporation.* New York: Praeger, 1973.

La Feber, Walter. *America, Russia, and the Cold War, 1945-1966.* New York: John Wiley and Sons, Inc., 1967.

Laqueur, Walter, Ed. *The Arab-Israeli Reader.* New York: Bantam, 1976.

———. *Confrontation: The Middle East and World Politics.* New York: Quadrangle, 1974.

———. *A History of Zionism.* New York: Holt, Rinehart and Winston, 1972.

———. *The Struggle for the Middle East: The Soviet Union in the Mediterranean, 1958-1968.* London: Routledge and Kegan Paul, 1970.

Lenczowski, George, Ed. *Middle East Oil in a Revolutionary Age.* Washington: American Enterprise Institute, March 1976.

———. *Political Elites in the Middle East.* Washington: American Enterprise Institute, 1973.

———. *Soviet Advance in the Middle East.* Washington: American Enterprise Institute, 1973.

Lenin, V.I. *Imperialism: The Highest Stage of Capitalism.* New York: International Publishers, 1939.

Levin, N. Gordon Jr. *Woodrow Wilson and World Politics.* New York: Oxford University Press, 1970.

Littauer, Raphael and Norman Uphoff. *The Air War in Indochina.* Boston: Beacon Press, 1972.

Logos, Gustavo and Horacio Godoy. *Revolution of Being: A Latin American View of the Future.* New York: The Free Press, 1978.

Long, David E. *The Persian Gulf.* Boulder, Colo.: Westview, 1976.

Maccoby, Michael. *The Corporate Individual.* New York: Simon and Schuster, 1975.

Magdoff, Harry. *The Age of Imperialism.* New York: Monthly Review Press, 1969.

Marcuse, Herbert. *One Dimensional Man.* Boston: Beacon Press, 1964.

———. *Repressive Tolerance.* Boston: Beacon Press, 1967.

Marshall, Charles B. *The Limits of Foreign Policy.* New York: Holt, 1954.

Marx, Karl and Frederick Engels. *The German Ideology.* New York: International Publishers, 1970.

May, Ernest. *American Imperialism: A Speculative Essay.* New York: Atheneum, 1968.

McNamara, Robert S. *The Essence of Security.* New York: Harper and Row Pubs., Inc., 1968.

Melman, Seymour. *Pentagon Capitalism.* New York: McGraw-Hill Book Co., 1970.

———. *The Permanent War Economy.* New York: Simon and Schuster, 1974.

Merk, Frederick. *Manifest Destiny and Mission in American History: A Reinterpretation.* New York: Knopf, 1963.

Midesell, Raymond F. *U.S. Private and Government Investment Abroad.* Oregon: University of Oregon, 1962.

Miliband, Ralph. *The State in Capitalist Society.* New York: Basic Books, 1969.

Moom, Parker T. *Imperialism and World Politics.* New York: Macmillan, 1926.

Morgan, Lewis H. *Ancient Society: Researches in the Lines of Human Progress from Savagery Through Barbarism to Civilization.* Chicago: C.H. Kerr, 1877.

Morganthou, Hans H. *In Defense of the National Interest.* New York: Knopf, 1951.

———. *Politics Among Nations.* New York: Knopf, 1967.

Morris, Bernard S. *Imperialism and Revolution.* Indiana: Indiana University Press, 1973.

Mosley, Leonard. *Power Plan: The Tumultuous World of Middle East Oil, 1890-1973.* London: Weidenfeld and Nicolson, 1973.

———. *Power Play: Oil in the Middle East,* Baltimore, Maryland: Penguin Books, Inc., 1973.

Mowry, George E. *The Era of Theodore Roosevelt and Birth of Modern America: 1900-1912.* New York: Harper & Row Pubs., Inc., 1964.

Muller, Ronald. *The Political Economy of Direct Foreign Investment.* Washington, D.C.: Inter-American Development Bank, July, 1970.

———. *The Relationship Between Foreign Trade and Economic Development: A Theoretical and Econometric Investigation.* Ph. D. Dissertation: The American University, 1970.

Neal, Fred Warner. *Titoism in Action.* Berkeley, Calif.: University of California Press, 1958.

———. *U.S. Foreign Policy and the Soviet Union.* Santa Barbara, Calfi.: Center for the Study of Democratic Institutions, 1961.

Nelson, R. and T.P. Schultz. *Structural Change in a Developing Economy.* Princeton: Princeton University Press, 1971.

Nirumand, Bahman. *Iran: The New Imperialism in Action.* New York: Monthly Review Press, 1969.

Nixon, Richard. *U.S. Foreign Policy for the 1970's: A New Strategy for Peace.* Washington, D.C.: Government Printing Office, 1970.

———. *U.S. Foreign Policy for the 1970's: Building for Peace.* Washington, D.C.: Government Printing Office, 1971.

Nutting, Anthony. *Nasser.* New York: E.P. Dutton, 1972.

O'Conner, Harvey. *World Crisis in Oil.* New York: Monthly Review Press, 1962.

O'Neill, Bard E. *Revolutionary Warfare in the Middle East: The Israelis Vs. The Fedayeen.* Boulder, Colo.: Paladin Press, 1974.

Osgood, Charles E. *Limited War.* Chicago: University of Chicago Press, 1957.

Osgood, Robert E. *Ideals and Self-Interest in America's Foreign Relations.* Chicago: University of Chicago Press, 1953.

Owen, Roger and Bob Sutcliff, Eds. *Studies in the Theory of Imperialism.* London: Longman Group Limited, 1972.

Parenti, Michael. *Trends and Tragedies in American Foreign Policy.* Boston: Little, Brown and Co., 1971.

Pearton, Maurice and John Stanley. *The International Trade in Arms.* New York: Praeger Publishers, 1971.

Penrose, Edith. *The Large International Firm in Developing Countries: The International Petroleum Industry.* Cambridge: MIT Press, 1968.

Peretz, Don. *The Middle East Today.* New York: Holt, Rinehart, and Winston, 1978.

Pettigrew, Richard F. *Imperial Washington.* New York: Arno Press, 1922.

P.J.D. Wiles. *Communist International Economies.* New York: Frederick A. Praeger, 1969.

Polk, William R. *The United States and the Arab World.* Cambridge: MIT Press, 1969.

———. *The United States and the Arab World.* Third Ed. Cambridge: Harvard University Press, 1975.

Pomerance, Michla. "American Guarantees to Israel and the Law of American Foreign Relations," Jerusalem Papers on Peace Problems No. 9, Jerusalem: The Hebrew University, December, 1974.

Pomeroy, William J. *American Neo-Colonialism: Its Emergence in the Philippines and Asia.* New York: International Publishers, 1970.

Pranger, Robert J. "American Policy for Peace in the Middle East, 1969-1971." Washington: American Enterprise Institute, 1973.

Pratt, Julius. *Expansionists of 1898: The Acquisition of Hawaii and the Spanish Islands.* Magnolia, Mass.: Peter Smith, Inc., 1936.

Raymond, Jack. *Power in the Pentagon.* New York: Harper & Row Pubs., Inc., 1964.

Reich, Bernard. *The Quest for Peace.* New York: Transaction Books, 1977.

Reisman, Michael. *The Art of the Possible: Diplomatic Alternatives in the Middle East.* Princeton: Princeton University Press, 1970.

Reuber, Grant. *Private Foreign Investment in Development.* London: Oxford University Press, 1973.

Rhodes, Robert I., Ed. *Imperialism and Underdevelopment.* New York: Modern Reader, 1972.

———. *Imperialism and Underdevelopment: A Reader.* New York: Monthly Review Press, 1970.

Robbins, Sidney and Robert Stobaugh. *Money in the Multinational Enterprise: A Study of Financial Policy*. New York: Basic Books, 1973.

Robock, Stefan and Kenneth Simmonds. *International Business and Multinational Enterprises*. Homewood, Ill.: Richard Irwin, 1973.

Rodinson, Maxime. *Israel: A Colonial-Settler State?* New York: Monad Press, 1973.

———. *Israel and the Arabs*. Baltimore: Penguin, 1973.

Rolfe, Sidney and Walter Damm. *The Multinational Corporation in the World Economy: Direct Investment in Perspective*. New York: Praeger.

Rose, Steven J. and James R. Kurth. *Testing Theories of Economic Imperialism*. Lexington, Mass.: D.C. Heath and Co., 1974.

Rostow, Eugene V. *The Middle East: Critical Choices for the United States*. Boulder, Colo.: Westview, 1977.

Rostow, Walt W. *The Stages of Economic Growth*. Cambridge: Cambridge University Press, 1969.

Safran, Nadav. *From War to War, 1948-1967*. New York: Pegasus, 1969.

Said, Abdul and Luiz Simmons. *The New Sovereigns: Multinational Corporations As World Powers*. New York: Spectrum, 1975.

Samelson, Neil J. *Karl Marx on Society and Social Change*. Chicago, Ill.: The University of Chicago Press, 1973.

Samir, Amin. *Accumulation on a World Scale: A Critique of the Theory of Underdevelopment, Two Volumes*. New York: Monthly Review Press, 1973.

Sampson, Anthony. *The Arms Bazaar from Lebanon to Lockheed*. New York: The Viking Press, 1977.

———. *The Seven Sisters: The Great Oil Companies and the World They Made*. New York: Viking Press, 1975.

———. *The Sovereign State of ITT*. New York: Fawcett, 1974.

Schonfield, Andrew. *Modern Capitalism*. New York: Oxford University Press, 1965.

Schumpeter, Joseph. *Imperialism and Social Classes*. New York: Augustus M. Kelley, Inc., 1951.

Schurmann, Franz. *The Logic of World Power: An Inquiry into the Origins, Currents and Contradictions of World Politics*. New York: Pantheon Books, 1974.

Schurr, Sam H. *Middle East Oil and the Western World, Prospects and Problems*. New York: American Elsevier, 1971.

Sid-Ahmed, Mohamed. *After the Guns Fall Silent*. New York: St. Martin's Press, 1977.

Sklar, Richard. *Corporate Power in an African State: The Political Impact of Multinational Mining Companies in Zambia*. Berkeley: University of California Press, 1975.

Smith, Donald E., Ed. *Religion, Politics, and Social Change in the Third World*. Riverside, New Jersey: The Free Press, 1971.

Snetsinger, John. *Truman, the Jewish Vote and the Creation of Israel*. Stanford, Calif.: Hoover Institute Press, 1974.

Sorensen, Theodore. *Kennedy*. New York: Harper & Row Pub., Inc., 1965.

Sprietsma, Cargill. *We Imperialists: Notes on Ernest Sullieres' Philosophy of Imperialism*. New York: AMS Press, Inc., 1967.

Stephens, Robert. *Nasser: A Political Biography*. New York: Simon and Schuster, 1971.

Stoessinger, John G. *Henry Kissinger: The Anguish of Power*. New York: Norton, 1976.

Stork, Joe. *Middle East Oil and the Energy Crisis*. New York: Monthly Review Press, 1975.

Tahtinen, Dale R. "The Arab-Israeli Military Balance Since 1973." Washington: American Enterprise Institute, 1974.

———. "Arab-Israeli Military Status in 1976." Washington: American Enterprise Institute, January, 1976.

Tanzer, Michael. *The Political Economy of International Oil and the Underdeveloped Countries.* Boston: Beacon Press, 1969.

Taylor, Alice. *Focus on the Middle East*. New York: Praeger Publishers, 1971.

Tekoah, Yosef. *In the Face of the Nations: Israel's Struggle for Peace*. New York: Simon and Schuster, 1976.

Tendler, Judith. *Inside Foreign Aid*. Baltimore: John Hopkins University Press, 1977.

Teodori, Massimo. *The New Left: A Documentary History*. New York: Bobbs-Merrill, 1969.

Trebling, Harry, Ed. *The Corporation in the American Economy*. Baltimore: John Hopkins University Press, 1971.

Tuma, Elias H. *Peacemaking and the Immoral War: Arabs and Jews in the Middle East*. New York: Harper & Row Pubs,. Inc,. 1972.

Turki, Fawaz. *The Disinherited: Journal of a Palestinian Exile*. New York: Monthly Review Press, 1972.

Turner, Louis. *Invisible Empires*. New York: Harcourt, Brace, and Jovanovich, 1971.

———. *Multinational Companies and the Third World*. New York: Hill and Wang, 1973.

Walton, Richard F. *Cold War and Counterrevolution: The Foreign Policy of John F. Kennedy*. New York: The Viking Press.

Weinstein, James. *The Corporate Ideal in the Liberal State: 1900-1918*. Boston: Beacon Press, 1975.

Wells, Alan. *Picture Tube Imperialism? The Impact of U.S. Television on Latin America.* Maryknoll, New York: Orbis Books, 1972.

Weston, Rubin F. *Racism in U.S. Imperialism*. Columbia, South Carolina: University of South Carolina, 1972.

Wilbur, Charles K. *Political Economy of Development and Underdevelopment*. New York: Random House, 1973.

Williams, William Appleman. *The Roots of Modern American Empire*. New York: Random House, 1969.

———. *Some Presidents: From Wilson to Nixon*. New York: New York Review of Books, 1972.

———. *The Tragedy of American Diplomacy*. New York: Delta, 1962.

Wills, Garry. *Nixon Agonistes*. New York: A Signet Book, 1970.

Winslow, E.M. *The Pattern of Imperialism*. New York: Columbia University Press, 1948.

Wolf, Charles Jr. *United States Policy and the Third World*. Boston: Little, Brown and Co., 1967.

Wright, Harrison M., Ed. *The New Imperialism: Analysis of Late Nineteenth Century Expansion.* Boston: D.C. Heath & Co., 1961

Wright, Quincy. *Mandates Under the League of Nations.* Chicago: University of Chicago Press, 1930.

Yost, Charles. *The Insecurity of Nations.* New York: Praeger Publishers, 1968.

INDEX

B

C

F

G

H

I

J

K

L

M

N

O

W

Y